Windows 8

A Step By Step Guide For Beginners:

Discover the Secrets to Unleash the Power of Windows 8!

Disclaimer

What Will You Find In This Report

If you love mobile devices, there's no reason you should not switch to this amazing new product from Microsoft. This report gives you all you need to know to start using Windows 8 with ease. The best part is that you can use the tips and tricks mentioned here to get the most of Windows 8 on your laptop, PC or a touchscreen device. Treat this report as an ultimate reference as it covers all the topics related to Windows 8 in an easy to understand style. So if there's anything that leaves you stumped, this report is your companion to pull you out of trouble. Let's get started and see how you can start using Windows 8.

Contents

Windows 8 1

A Step By Step Guide For Beginners: 1

Discover the Secrets to Unleash the Power of Windows 8! 1

Disclaimer 2

What Will You Find In This Report 3

Introduction – Windows 8 "Only Gets Better" 7

Chapter One: Getting Started 11

See How You Can Get Windows 8 11

Why Should You Upgrade to Windows 8? 16

Starting and Ending a Session 20

Chapter Two: It's Time to Explore Windows 8 23

Get to Know the Windows Charms 23

Customize the Start Screen 26

The Language of Touch 30

Using the Taskbar 33

Time to Have a Look at the Desktop 36

Accessing Files and Settings 37

Working with the Control Panel 40

Get to Know the Power Plans 41

Organizing Files and Folders 43

Networking Basics 47

Protecting Your Windows 51

Data Backup and Restoring Files 54

Chapter Three: Make the Apps Work 61

How to Use Built-in Apps 61

Can You Use Two Apps Together? 62

Switching Between Apps 63

Exploring Accessories and Tools 64

Fun with Multimedia...65

Building Your Own Applications...66

Using Live Tiles...67

SkyDrive and Social Apps..68

Chapter Four: The All New "Windows Store" – Your Personal Dashboard 72

Shopping in the Windows Store 72

Exploring and Obtaining Apps..73

Chapter Five: Windows 8 and Security Features...74

Chapter Six: What's so new in Windows 8? 77

Windows Store...77

Microsoft Account and Cloud Connection...78

Internet Explorer 10...79

Family Safety Settings...80

Virus and Malware protection...81

Windows 8 Interface...82

Online Storage and SkyDrive..83

Windows Reader...84

Integrated Social Networks...85

Chapter Seven: Hardware and Device Compatibility 86

Windows 8 Gives You More Flexibility...87

Give Your Device a Longer life..88

Connect and Share Between Devices...89

Chapter Eight: How Can You Move Your Stuff on Windows 8? 90

Moving files and settings from another PC – Windows Easy Transfer 90

What is Windows Easy Transfer?..90

What Can You Transfer?...90

What are the Supported Formats?..90

What Transfer Methods Can You Use?...91

Preparing for File Transfer 92

Are There Any Problems? 93

Chapter Nine: The Cloud Connection – Your Contacts and Documents are Everywhere! 94

You Can Do Great Things with Windows 8 Cloud Connection 94

Stay Connected to your files 24/7 96

What is SkyDrive? 97

What does SkyDrive do? 98

How Can You Transfer Your Files to the Cloud Directly? 102

How Can You Access SkyDrive? 104

Chapter Ten: Windows 8 for Business 105

How is Windows 8 Useful for Businesses? 106

Chapter Eleven: Internet Explorer 10 – Redefine Browser Possibilities 107

Basic Navigation 109

Additional Features 110

Pinning Websites to the Start Screen 111

Web Tracking Protection 114

The Internet Explorer 10 on Desktop 116

Chapter Twelve: Keeping Your Windows 8 "Up to Date" 118

Updating Windows 8 Drivers 120

Finding the Right Drivers 122

Moving from Windows 8 to Windows 8 Pro 123

Chapter Thirteen: Tips for Improving Your Windows 8 Experience 124

Advanced Options 132

Third-Party Apps 133

Keyboard Shortcuts 134

Deleting Files 136

Chapter Fourteen: Conclusion – What More Can You Expect? 137

Kindle Fire HD: How to Use Your Tablet With Ease: The Ultimate Guide to Getting Started, Tips, Tricks, Applications and More 138

Introduction – Windows 8 "Only Gets Better"

Welcome to the world of Windows 8 and you can rest assured that your experience will only get better. On October 26th, 2012, Windows 8 was made available as an exciting operating system for mobile devices. If you compare this product to other Windows operating systems, you'll see that significant changes have been made to the existing operating system interface to enhance your experience. Yes, Windows 8 can be used on laptops, PCs, tablets and even smartphones.

Most of you are probably familiar with popular Windows products such as Windows XP, Windows Vista and Windows 7. Although Microsoft has made several improvements in the operating system over the years, nothing beats the excitement of the Windows 8 experience. The fast and fluid design is perfect for large PCs and 'compact' touch enabled devices. You can do more in less time when you browse through Windows 8 as it gives you instant access to your contacts, applications and documents.

You'll also love browsing through the All New "Windows Store", and more details are coming up in the later chapters. Moreover, those of you who are interested in downloading exciting apps would be pleased to see the wide collection of useful apps including apps to help you with work and of course, the latest games.

What's even more amazing is the fact that a number of apps can work together. So you can now share photos, videos, documents, contacts, links, and lots more really easily. In short, whatever you want to get done can be done quickly with Windows 8.

Wonder how this is possible? Windows 8 is linked to the cloud and you can also use touch, mouse, and keyboard together. Your operating system is connected to the cloud which means you can access all your important documents, photos and files from any PC, laptop or device having Windows 8.

In addition to a new look, you can expect many more rock solid features from Windows 8. The desktop is similar to one used in Windows 7, but everything you considered great when using Windows 7 only gets better with this latest version of Windows operating system. This includes security, desktop applications, customization and settings.

Windows 8 will open on its lock screen.
If you have no clues about what to do next, simply tap the space bar, spin your mouse wheel or swipe upwards on your touch screen to reveal a familiar login

---

The new Start screen in Windows 8 shows you everything in one place. You'll find more information about customizing the start screen later in this report, but for now get ready for fun because Windows 8's start screen has all the information you require in one place. Yes, your appointments, calendar, contacts, weather updates, favorite playlists, photo albums, websites and preferred apps are placed right at the center. Moreover, viewing and interacting with your start screen is faster than ever and you can also decide how you want to place the items on the start screen.

Windows 8 uses 'Live' tiles that update in real time so that you can stay on top of your appointments. Pictures and files can be shared with the help of a couple of clicks and getting updates about news, sports and your friend's status had never been this easy and quick. With Windows 8, you can launch your favorite apps, switch between different tasks, and browse through files and folders literally without 'digging' for information. It's all right there on one screen right at start and most importantly in your own personal style.

If you are a Windows 7 user, you will be greeted with a familiar desktop as some settings and features you used earlier are still there in Windows 8. This latest offering from Microsoft should be your choice if you want to get things done immediately.

The seamless integration of touch, mouse and keyboard gives you a chance to work and play at the same time. So whether you want to read a book, play a game or create a business presentation, you can do everything at once with the enhanced features of Windows 8. Putting it simply, do whatever you think is the right approach at that point in time.

Life is going to get a lot easier for those of you who have touch-enabled PCs. Things you used to do with a physical mouse and keyboard can now be done with touch. With the help of a touch keyboard you can browse through apps, navigate web pages and interact with live tiles on the go.

The touch keyboard in Windows 8 has two modes that are specially designed to suit your style. You can either work with a large keyboard displayed on your screen with large buttons or go for one that is split on either sides of the screen. Choose a style you are more comfortable with. Remember, typing is going to be natural and smooth no matter if you are walking around with your device or are sitting down in one place.

This discussion was only a slight glimpse of what you are going to get. Windows 8 has many more interesting features you cannot afford to miss. Continue reading to know more about how you can get Windows 8 and how it can help you.

Chapter One: Getting Started

See How You Can Get Windows 8

If you are really interested to install Windows 8 on your PC or laptop, you need to first identify whether or not the product is compatible with your system. Microsoft has outlined the following minimum requirements for their latest product.

1 GHz CPU, the graphics chipset you use should be capable of running DirectX 9

Screen resolution of 1024 x 768

1 GB of RAM and 16 GB of hard drive space for 32 bit version

2 GB of RAM and 20 GB of hard drive space if you are going for 64 bit version

Note: You can upgrade to Windows 8 without trouble if you are using Windows 7 or Windows Vista on your hardware.

In addition to your system, your favorite applications, programs and laptop/PC peripheral devices also need to be compatible with Windows 8. To do so, you can visit the Windows Compatibility center at http://www.microsoft.com/en-us/windows/compatibility

All you have to do here is type the name of your printer, keyboard or any other PC accessory to see whether it will work with Windows 8. You will also be given useful links to driver software in some cases. This additional software needs to be downloaded before your accessory starts working. If you want to upgrade to Windows 8, make a list of devices you use and check their compatibility before you switch to the newer operating system. This isn't a tough call. Here are some useful tricks to help you make a list of devices you intend to use.

For Windows XP Users

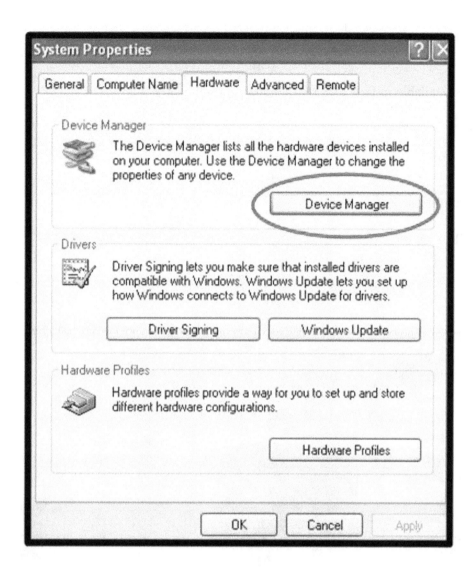

Right click *My Computer* and select *Properties*. Click *Hardware* tab and go to **Device Manager**.

For Windows Vista and Windows 7 Users

Click *Start*, type **device manager** in the search bar, and then hit **<Enter>**.

Note: You don't have to verify all your devices, but make sure that your display, audio, and devices used for networking are compatible with Windows 8.

Which Version of Windows 8 Should I Get?

Windows 8 is available in four different versions namely:

Windows 8

Windows 8 Pro

Windows 8 Enterprise

Windows 8 RT

As the name suggests, Windows 8 Enterprise is specifically meant for use by business enterprises. Windows 8 RT is specially designed for Windows tablets, so as PC or laptop owner, you are left with only two options.

You can either go for Windows 8 or install Windows 8 Pro. What's the difference between the two? Windows 8 Pro includes a few extra features that are only useful for serious PC users. You get BitLocker encryption and the ability to use the Remote Desktop when you get Windows 8 Pro version. Windows 8 should be your choice if you want to keep things simple.

Should I Upgrade to Windows 8 or get a fresh Install Done?

If you are running a Professional or Ultimate version of Windows 7 and want to keep your important data untouched, the only option available to you is to upgrade to Windows 8 Pro. A fresh install should be your choice if you are not really interested to save any information on your hardware.

Windows 8 upgrade is really simple and quick. Moreover, it also saves time as Windows will automatically save your applications and data files for later use. You can go for updates but remember that there are additional costs. You'll have lots of excess baggage in the form of data and application backup that only takes up space on your hard drive.

Remember the choice is yours and you are in a better position to decide whether you want a fresh install or prefer to upgrade your product.

Why Should You Upgrade to Windows 8?

If you are still not sure whether or not you should upgrade to Windows 8, here is a brief discussion to help you make a good decision. You'll surely switch to this innovative operating system once you finish reading the next few pages.

There's no other OS that performs so well!

Why download Windows 8?

It goes where you go

Your pictures, files, and settings are easily synced through the cloud, so you can get to what you need almost anywhere.

It plays as hard as it works

Windows 8 gives you the power to quickly browse, watch movies, play games, polish your resume, and pull together a killer presentation—all on a single PC.

You keep all your files

If your PC is running Windows 7, your files, apps, and settings will easily transfer to Windows 8.

You keep familiar programs

Programs that run on Windows 7 will run on Windows 8.

Most people go out and buy products only after reading excellent reviews and the case is no different for small business owners. If this is the time you want to get a new laptop or PC, you can go for the latest operating system launched by Microsoft. For those of you who are still running Windows XP, Vista or Windows 7, the upgrade task should be a simple task. And, there's a reason to switch too. Windows 8 will definitely perform better than your existing OS even on the same hardware, so why not make the change?

Always Stay Connected

This report does mention that Windows 8 is connected to the cloud and you need to keep this in mind. Once you log into Windows 8 using your Microsoft Account, your apps and personal preferences will automatically be synced to the cloud. This means if you decide to change your system and install Windows 8 on your new device, you don't need to worry about your previous settings.

Those settings and preferences you used on your old system can automatically be downloaded so that you can enjoy the same experience no matter which device you use.

The New and Improved "Refresh / Reset" Features

The Refresh option in Windows 8 makes your life easier as it gives you a "fresh" start. Basically this Refresh tool allows Windows 8 to reinstall on your system automatically. During the process, Windows 8 saves your personal files and apps you've downloaded from the Windows Store. Some of your most important settings are also saved along with your user account configurations.

After your computer gets a refreshed copy of Windows 8, you only need to reinstall your desktop programs. What's really appreciable about Windows 8 is the fact that you will find a list of programs installed on your previous version with their complete website links right on your desktop. Go through the list to see the programs you need to reinstall.

Refresh is especially useful if you want to sort your applications. Since you get a list of programs you need to reinstall, you can skip ones that are causing problems or you no longer need them.

The Reset feature in Windows 8 is more severe when it comes to cleaning your copy. This is a good option if you plan to resell your system or want to donate your PC to someone else. Basically, your Windows 8 copy will be returned to the same version you received when you started using your product for the first time. Your user account details or apps will not be saved, so nothing much is left.

You'll Never Run Short of Storage Spaces

Have you ever run out of storage space on your hard drive? Most of you will probably say yes as this is not something unusual. Storage space does become a serious issue when you have to store large amounts of media such as photos and video clips.

Well, you do find a number of storage space solutions these days under the name of removable external storage, but they have their own set of pros and cons. If your external storage device crashes, you could be left with no other option than to regret limited storage space on your system.

Windows 8 solves your storage dilemma as you will never run out of space. In addition to a reliable cloud connection, it also uses a software-based system known as RAID to protect your important data and files. This system also ensures that your data remains undamaged even if there's a hardware failure.

Protect Your Data from Corruption and Accidental Loss

Accidental loss, changes, deletion and corruption of data presents a great deal of problems, but Windows 8 has a number of helpful tools to protect your important data. One of the best features of Windows 8 is the periodic scanning of critical file locations such as Desktop, Contacts,

Favorites and Libraries. You will be notified every time your operating system identifies a change.

File History in Windows 8 maintains a complete history of the changes made to your data over time. With this option, you can easily go back in time and reverse all the changes that are unwanted.

Hope this discussion helps ease your transition to Windows 8. However, you will come across a number of other attractive reasons that will clear your doubts about moving to this new, innovative operating system from Microsoft as you continue reading this report.

Starting and Ending a Session

If you are using Windows 8 on your laptop or PC, there is no need to shutdown your system completely to end a session. You can put your PC or laptop in sleep mode and this has a number of advantages.

First, your PC or laptop uses little power and it also starts up faster. You can instantly go back to the point where you left your session which means there is no need to reopen your documents or browser window. Just in case your battery gets very low, Windows 8 automatically saves your work and shuts down your PC or laptop.

Note: For most laptops, you only have to close the lid to put your system in the sleep mode. In case of tablets and other touch devices, you have to press the power button to put your device to sleep.

Here are some quick tips you can use to set sleep mode as the default action when you press the power button on your device.

Open the Search charm in Windows 8 and enter power in the search box. (Do check out the next section to know how you can access the charms).

Tap/click Settings that appears on the right and then go to Power options.

If you are using a tablet or desktop computer, select Sleep for what you want the power button to do. Once you have made the relevant changes, tap/click Save changes before you exit the dialog box.

You can change the settings for your laptop as well and the process is not very different. Choose what closing the lid would do to your laptop both when you are using the laptop battery and when your laptop is plugged in. You can then save your changes and exit the dialog box.

Note: If you don't want to use your tablet, laptop or PC for a while, you can choose to shut down your system completely. As a Windows 8 user, you need to learn how to shut down your system completely because the new operating system lacks the traditional 'Windows' Start button.

More information on exciting and strange features in Windows 8 can be found in the upcoming pages, but presently let's find out how you can shut down your session completely on Windows 8.

Drag your mouse to the lower right or upper left corner of your screen to access the Charms bar. You can also access the Charms bar using the swipe and slide action of Windows 8. Holding Win key + C would also take you to the Charms bar.

Tap/ click Settings and then hit the Power button.

Click or tap your desired option from the given choices *Sleep*, *Shut down*, or *Update and restart.*

If you want to shut down your PC, close any apps or documents you have open. You will be asked to save your work in case you have made any changes.

Tap or click Shut down to close your system completely.

Chapter Two: It's Time to Explore Windows 8

Get to Know the Windows Charms

No matter how busy you are, the charm bar in Windows 8 helps you do the things you like to do very easily. You can search for files, share your favorite links and change your device settings with the useful charms that appear in the latest product from Microsoft. Before moving ahead, there is something you need to keep in mind. The five charms in Windows 8 work differently when you're on the Start screen or are using your favorite app.

The five charms in Windows 8 include:

Search allows you to search for anything. This means you can find a specific message in your email or look for a specific app or file on your laptop or PC.

Sharing files, photos and information with others gets really easy with **Share**. You can also email photos, videos to your family or update your Facebook status using the same charm.

Start helps you get back to your Start screen. In case you're already on the Start screen, you can use this charm to go back to the last application you were using.

Devices lists all the devices connected to your system (also includes wireless devices). You can use this charm to print files or stream your favorite movie on your TV.

As the name suggests, **Settings** allows you to customize settings for Windows 8**.** You'll find useful info for changing settings of apps you're using. Moreover, common PC setting such as network connections, volume, screen display and brightness, notification management, power options, and keyboard can also be changed using this charm.

You'll always find the charms on the right side of your screen. Here's how you can open any charm in Windows 8.

For touch devices:

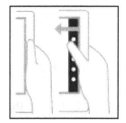

Swipe towards the left from the right edge of your screen and tap the charm you want.

For Laptops and PCs:

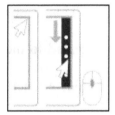

Drag your mouse to the right edge of your screen and move the pointer into the upper or lower right corner of the screen. Move your mouse up or down to access the charms bar and click the one you want.

Customize the Start Screen

In pretty much every version of Windows, you would double 'click' the items to open them and hit your mouse button an infinite number of times to customize your desktop. The intriguing approach adopted by Windows 8 eliminates all the hassles to make your life easier. This modern system can also be used on touch centric devices that have become an integral part of our lives.

What really makes the Windows 8 experience so fascinating is the fact that your apps are easily accessible and you don't have to create a number of "Shortcuts" on your desktop. This means getting around your favorite apps and documents is faster and more efficient compared to the earlier version of Windows and this latest offering is specially designed to accommodate touch, keyboard and mouse at the same time.

The Modern user interface offered by Windows 8 is not only pretty, but it is more efficient and offers faster navigation than any other previous versions of Windows. Well, most of you would be shocked to know that there is no traditional Start button in Windows 8. This might come as a surprise because we have become so used to the Start Menu.

So how does your Windows 8 Start Screen really look? Your screen will have a sea of tiles, but the look is more aesthetically pleasing than the previous operating systems launched by Microsoft. There's a lot you can do with the Live tiles and the best part is that you can easily group and shuffle applications according to your personal preferences. This greatly simplifies your life because you don't have to hunt several folders to access what you actually need to use at that point in time.

Those of you who are excited to know more, you have a lively Start screen in Windows 8. All information you really care about can be put in one place. This means your favorite apps, websites, contacts and folders will be available on one screen.

Here are the quickest ways to customize your Start screen.

If you are using a touch device, simply swipe from the right edge of your screen and move your finger towards the left. Tap Start from the menu that appears on the side of the screen.

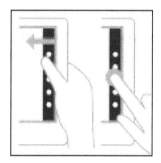

If you are using a mouse, move your cursor to the upper or lower right corner of your screen. Move upwards and click **Start** from the menu that appears on the screen.

If you are using a keyboard, press the Windows logo key to access Start.

Once you access the Start screen, you can arrange it in any way you want. The best thing to do would be to put your favorite apps, contacts, websites and folders right in the center. Here a few tricks you can use to make your Start screen look the best.

Create tiles for your favorite apps on the Start screen

A live tile is an application you can open from the start screen directly. If you visit a website daily or want to chat with your friend all the time, consider creating tiles for them on the start screen so that you can go to them without wasting much time.

How You Can Create Live Tiles

If there's a contact, website or application you want to add to Start, open the **"App Command"** and tap/click **Pin to Start.**

If you want to pin a folder, you have to first open it using File Explorer. Press and hold the folder if you are using touch devices or right click it when using a laptop or PC. You can tap or click **Pin to Start** to place the tile on your Start screen.

How You Can Access App Command

To access App Command on a touch device, swipe up from the bottom edge of the screen or swipe down from the top of the screen. Tap the command you want to select at the moment.

On a laptop or a PC, all you have to do is right-click within the app or folder. Then click the command you want to select.

How You Can Pin and Unpin Apps from the Start

The apps you install on your PC, laptop or touch devices can be pinned to Start if you want them to be present there. Just find the app using the Search charm, open its commands and then tap/click **Pin to Start**.

Similarly, if your Start screen has apps you no longer use, you have the option to "Unpin" them. If you want to unpin an application, open its commands and then tap/click **Unpin from Start**. This only removes the app from your start screen and you can continue using it as it will not be uninstalled from your system.

How You Can Rearrange and Resize Tiles

It's really easy to move and rearrange tiles on the Windows 8 Start screen. If you want to move a Live tile, first drag it up or down, then move it to your desired location. You can arrange the tiles whichever way you want and it is always good to group your favorites together in one place.

If you want to fit lots of tiles in one spot, you can make them larger or smaller depending on your situation. First select the tile on your start screen and then open its commands. Tap/click Larger or Smaller to change the size, however the size of every tile cannot be changed.

The Language of Touch

In Windows 8, things are even more simplified than what you think. If you want to know more about what this means, make sure you read through the next few pages. Touch, tap and swipe are three things you will master when you interact with Windows 8. Have a look at the following features to know how incredible this touch centric user interface actually is.

What Happens When You Tap?

When you tap once, the item you tap opens. This feature is quite similar to clicking the item (app/folder or document) with a mouse.

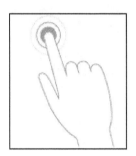

What Happens When You Press and Hold an Item?

When you press and hold an item on your screen for a few seconds, you'll be guided to a specific menu to tell you more about what you are doing. This action is very similar to right clicking the item with the mouse.

How Can You Stretch and Zoom an Item?

If you want to shrink or stretch an item on your screen, you can touch the item with two fingers and then move them in the direction intended. For example, move your fingers towards each other if you want to shrink or pinch the item. On the other hand, move your fingers away from each other if you want to enlarge the item. One of the best places to try the zoom feature is your very own Start screen.

How Can You Rotate an Item?

The touch interface used in Windows 8 gives you a chance to rotate a few items. Place two or more fingers on the item and then turn your hand in the direction you want.

Using the Slide Feature

Swiping from the Side of the Screen

Swiping from the right edge of your screen opens the charms bar. The bar contains five icons namely Search, Share, Start, Devices and Settings and you can select the icon you want to work with.

Similarly, when you swipe your finger from the left edge of your screen, you can see your open apps. If you want to close any application, drag the app to the bottom of the screen without lifting your finger.

Swiping from the bottom edge of the screen often brings up app commands.

How You Can Scroll Using Your Fingers

Scrolling a long distance on Windows 8 is not a difficult task as you only have to drag your finger in the direction intended on your touch screen. You can read through the entire document as this action is very similar to scrolling with a mouse.

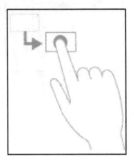

Rearranging Items

If you want to move an item to a new location, press and drag it using your finger until you reach the desired spot. The best part is that you can move the item in all directions and once you are happy with the new location, you can release your finger. A good place to explore more of this slide and drag action is your Windows 8 Start screen.

Note:

You need to use a touch screen to use the interactions mentioned above.

Using the Taskbar

Your Windows 8 taskbar can be found along the bottom of your desktop and serves as an ideal spot to launch your favorite programs. When you pin your favorite programs to the taskbar, you can keep them in sight and opening them is just one click away.

If you are not sure how you can get the most of your taskbar, there is nothing to worry about. Windows 8 allows you to customize your taskbar and this includes the way your taskbar will look, how your programs are grouped together and how do your apps and programs group together when you open more than one window. In short, you have the power to decide the items that will appear on your taskbar.

How Can I Rearrange the Taskbar Buttons?

All you have to do is drag the button from its current position and place it on the position you desire. You can rearrange the buttons on the taskbar as often as you like. There is something you need to keep in mind. If you open a number of files from one app, they will always be grouped together even if they were opened at different times. This gives you a chance to preview all the open files from the same app at the same time.

You Can Change the Position of Your Taskbar

Actually a taskbar is always found at the bottom of your desktop, but with Windows 8 you can actually move it to the top of your desktop and even the sides. Before you can move your taskbar, you need to unlock it first.

To unlock the taskbar, simply tap or click to remove the check mark that appears next to it. Once the check mark disappears, press and hold any empty space on your taskbar and drag the bar to one of the four edges where you want it to be positioned. After the taskbar is where you want it to be, release the hold.

How You Can Pin an App to the Taskbar

Windows 8 allows you to pin your favorite apps to the taskbar so that you can access them quickly.

To do this, first swipe your finger from the right edge of the screen to reveal the Charms bar. Tap/click Search to enter the name of the app you want to open.

Once the app is opened, press and hold or right-click the app's icon on the taskbar to open a dialog box.

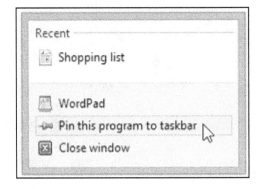

Tap/click **Pin this program to taskbar** to add the item to your Windows 8 taskbar.

To remove an app later, press and hold or right-click the app's icon on the taskbar and then tap/click **Unpin this program from taskbar.** Remember, this only removes the app from the taskbar and does not uninstall the program.

How You Can Customize the Notification Area in the Taskbar

The notification area can be found at the far right side of the taskbar and gives you status and updates about things like network (internet) connection, email, battery etc. You can customize the notification area and only place icons you want to access quite often.

If you want to hide an icon in the notification area, tap/click the icon first and then drag it towards the desktop. To add this item later, click the tiny **"Show hidden icons arrow"** and drag the icon back to the notification area. You can add as many hidden icons as you want to if you change your mind.

To rearrange icons that appear in the notification area, all you have to do is drag the icon that appears to any other spot. Remember, if you hide an icon, you will no longer receive notifications for that app.

Time to Have a Look at the Desktop

If you want to get to the desktop quickly without closing your running apps, you can use the **Show desktop button** at the right end of the taskbar. This allows you to preview the desktop without affecting the programs that are running. To get back to the Windows, you can tap/click the Show desktop button again.

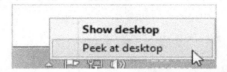

You can also "Peek at the Desktop" using the **Peek at desktop** button. First right-click the Show desktop button and then hit "Peek at desktop."

Accessing Files and Settings

Accessing important files on Windows 8 is possible with the help of File Explorer. You can open File Explorer (previously known as Windows Explorer) by swiping your finger from the right edge of your screen and then typing File Explorer in the search box. Just a friendly reminder, you have to first access 'Search' from the charms bar and then type File Explorer.

File Explorer Search Box

Depending on the number of files you have stored on your PC or laptop, it is never less than a daunting task to browse a number of folders to find the particular file you need. Windows 8 helps you save time, so there is a Search box to assist you in finding your files.

The search box can be found at the top of every window. To start looking for a particular file, tap or click the search box and enter a search term. You can enter the name of your file or stick to the starting letter. You will find display results based on the term you enter in the box. Files that match with the character you enter are filtered during the search process.

Using the Search charm to Find Files

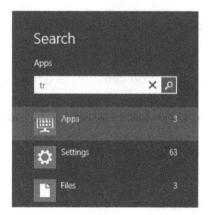

Access the charms bar by swiping in from the right edge of your screen.

Tap/click Search and then enter your search term.

To search for a particular app, setting, or file on your laptop or PC, tap or click Apps, Settings, or Files, whichever applies. You will then be guided to more refined results and you can then find your desired app or file.

You can directly press Windows logo key ⊞+F to search for a file if you are using a keyboard.

To open a particular location in File Explorer, you can enter the specific path directly in the Search charm. For example, if you enter C:\ in the search box, a list of files and folders contained on your C drive will appear on the screen. You can then browse the different folders to access the file you need.

How You Can Create and Delete a File

New files can be created easily by using an app. For example, you can create a new word document by using a word processing app such as Microsoft Word. Similarly, video or movie files can be created using a movie maker or any video recording app. Most apps installed on your PC or laptop save the newly created files in common locations such as My Documents, which makes it really easy for you as a user to find the files the next time you need them.

If you feel you no longer need the files, you can always delete it from your laptop or PC to save valuable disk space. To delete a file, you need to first find the file and then select it. Tap/click **Delete** to remove the file from your folder.

What Happens to the Files You Delete?

Once a file is deleted, it is moved to the Recycle bin where it is stored for some time. Actually, the Recycle Bin saves your files and folders that you may have deleted accidently. You can easily recover the files that you never wanted to delete in the first place. If you don't require anything from the Recycle Bin, you can empty the entire contents to free the storage space being used by the deleted files.

How You Can Recover and Remove Files from the Recycle Bin

Typically, files that are deleted from your PC are moved to the Recycle Bin and you can move them back to where they were.

To recover files from the Recycle Bin, double tap/click the Recycle Bin icon the desktop. If you are using File Explorer, enter Recycle Bin in the address bar to open the location (i.e. the Recycle Bin). To restore all the files in the Recycle Bin, tap/click the Recycle Bin tools tab first, and then hit Restore all items. The files will be automatically restored to their original places on your PC. If you want to restore selected files, select the desired files and then tap/ click Restore the selected items.

You can also choose to permanently delete your file if you don't want them to consume extra space on your Hard Drive. Open File Explorer and then go to the Recycle Bin. Choose Empty Recycle Bin to remove the files from your system. Remember, you cannot recover the files if you delete them permanently.

Working with the Control Panel

If you cannot find the Control Panel after you've installed Windows 8, there is no point in getting worried. The Control Panel is still there and you only need to find it. Getting hold of the control panel is really easy. First, swipe in from the right edge of your screen to access the Charms bar. Then tap/click Search followed by typing Control Panel in the search box. This should be it. Your Control Panel will then be sitting right in front of you on your screen.

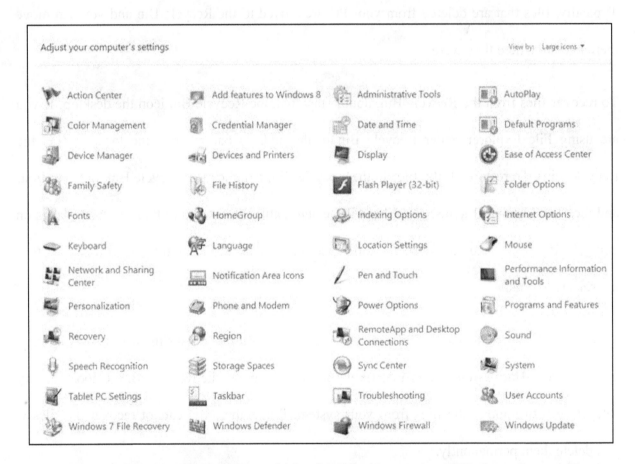

Most of the settings in Windows 8 would be familiar if you are a Windows 7 user. You can browse through individual components to check and change the settings for your system.

Get to Know the Power Plans

A power plan basically is a collection of settings to manage how your PC or laptop uses power. Power plans that are available to you depend on the kind of PC or laptop you have. Power options can be accessed from the Control Panel. Windows normally gives you the following power plans:

Balanced

This option offers 'full' performance when your PC or laptop needs it and saves power when you don't use your PC or laptop. Most experts suggest that this is the best power plan you can use.

Power saver

Power saver reduces the performance of your laptop or PC and screen brightness to save power. You can switch to power saver mode if you want to get the most of your single laptop battery.

High performance

As the name suggests, High performance gives you best PC performance and maximizes the brightness of your screen. Even though the performance of your computer improves, this plan uses a lot more power. So, don't be surprised if your laptop battery does not last long when you this option.

If you're using a laptop with Windows 8, you can click the battery icon 🔋 that appears in the notification area to choose a power plan. Remember, you can only choose from the options that are made available by your laptop manufacturer.

You can also create your own power plans by going to **Power Options > Create a Power Plan**

Create a power plan

To create your own plan, start by selecting one of the following plans that is closest to what you want.

◉ **Balanced (recommended)**
Automatically balances performance with energy consumption on capable hardware.

○ Power saver
Saves energy by reducing your computer's performance where possible.

○ High performance
Favors performance, but may use more energy.

Plan name:

My Custom Plan 1

[Next]   [Cancel]

Organizing Files and Folders

You are surely going to love Windows 8 more than ever because it gives you a chance to organize your files and folders without trouble. This should be some 'great news' if you are a sort of a person who has hundreds of files stored in an unimaginable number of different folders. The File Explorer in Windows 8 makes it easier to do lots of organizing really quickly.

Most of the common commands you need to organize your files are the Home and View tab of the File Explorer. You can now:

Copy, cut and paste files directly

Display files according to file extensions

Search for your important files using the date you last modified the file, the type of file and other properties.

The ribbon displaying Home and View tab is minimized by default, so the commands won't appear when you are not using them. If you want to keep the ribbon always open, tap /click a tab, and then tap/click the 'Pin icon' that appears on the far right of your screen.

The **Home** tab is normally used for copying and moving files. You can also use it to create new folders.

You can use the **View** tab to sort your files and folders and change the way they appear on your screen.

How You Can Organize Your Files and Folders

If you just don't know where to begin, here are a few tips and tricks to help you organize your files and folders.

Choose to preview the files. This way you can quickly spot the files you don't need and can get rid of them. You can select Preview pane from the main View tab for the purpose. When you select a file in Preview pane, you can take a peek at it which is faster than opening the file manually. If you find nothing useful in the file, send the file to the Recycle bin.

Sort your documents by date. This type of sorting reveals the old files that are no longer required. You can go ahead and delete the files to free valuable disk space.

You can also sort your files and documents by size. Delete the heaviest files that you no longer need to free up more space on your hard drive.

Similarly, files and folders can also be organized according to date. This is especially useful if you have important photos and videos related to a particular event. Remember, things can get messy when you store lots of photos and videos on your laptop or PC, so creating a folder for each date can save you lots of time.

You can always name similar files in the same way. For example, if you are sports fan and want to keep track of your favorite soccer team, you can create a folder named Sports with files named as soccer calendar, soccer photos and soccer players. Well, there are no rules you have to follow when naming the files. Try to stick to a pattern you can recognize easily to make your task easier.

How You Can Open a File

To open a file, all you have to do is double tap/click it. Your file will open in the same app that you used to create the file by default. For example, word documents in DOCX format automatically open using Microsoft Word.

If you want to change the default setting, you can select the file and then tap/click the Home tab. Move your finger/mouse pointer to tap/click the small arrow next to open. You will then see a list of apps displayed on your screen so select the app you want to use to open your file.

How You Can:

Rename Your Files and Folder

First select a file or folder and then tap/click the Home tab. Tap/click Rename and enter the new name for your file or folder.

Copy Files and Folders

Files and folders can be copied in a number of different ways in File Explorer.

You can either select the items you want to copy, tap/click the Home tab and then tap/click Copy or Cut. Selecting Copy copies the item and you can move the entire item to a new location when you select Cut. After you select Cut or Copy, open the new location and then tap/click Paste.

If you are using a keyboard, try shortcuts such as Ctrl+C to copy or Ctrl+X to cut files and folders. You can then go to the new location and press Ctrl+V to paste the files you've selected.

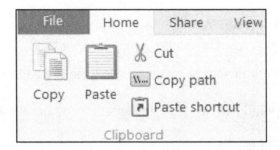

Use two File Explorer windows opened side by side and drag items from one window to the other window.

Networking Basics

Windows 8 is a lot different from other previous versions of Windows, but setting up an internet connection is not that difficult. You can follow these simple steps to connect to the internet and start browsing the web.

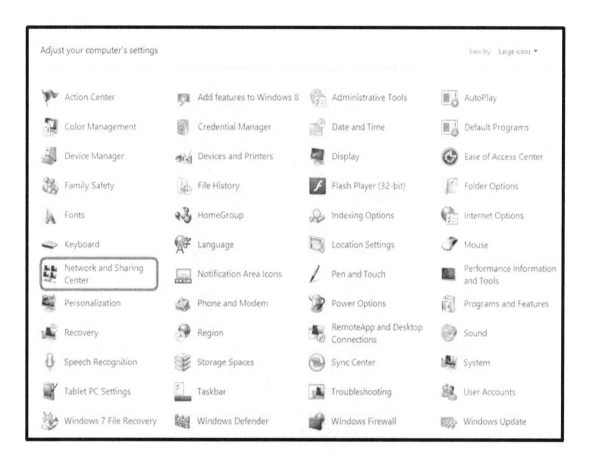

Move your mouse to the right edge of your screen or swipe in from the right side to access the Charms bar. Click the Search charm and enter Control Panel in the Search box. Once you reach the Control Panel, tap/click Network and Sharing Center to view the details about your available Network Connections.

Click/tap the connection you want to connect and you might be ready to start browsing the web. You will have to enter a password to connect to security enabled wireless connections.

Another way to connect to the internet using Windows 8 is directly using the Search bar. Your Windows 8 automatically searches for available connections and lists the ones that are available. To connect this way, first access the Charms bar and then tap/click Settings.

The network icon will appear as (📶 or 📲) depending on your surroundings. Tap/click the network icon. From the list of connections that appear, first tap/click the network you want to connect to, and then tap or click **Connect**.

If you connect to a wireless network, you will have to enter a password if the connection is security enabled. If you are connecting to an open or unsecured network, you can start browsing the web instantly.

When you add a new Wi-Fi network to your list of connections, Windows 8 will automatically connect to that network whenever it is in range. If you want to connect to another network, you will have to repeat the same steps you followed for connecting to the internet.

If you face any problems while connecting to the internet, you can always figure out a likely cause by visiting Network Diagnostics

First, move your mouse pointer or finger to access the Charms bar. Type Control Panel in the Search box and you will be guided to the Windows 8 Control Panel. Open Action Center and then tap/click Troubleshooting.

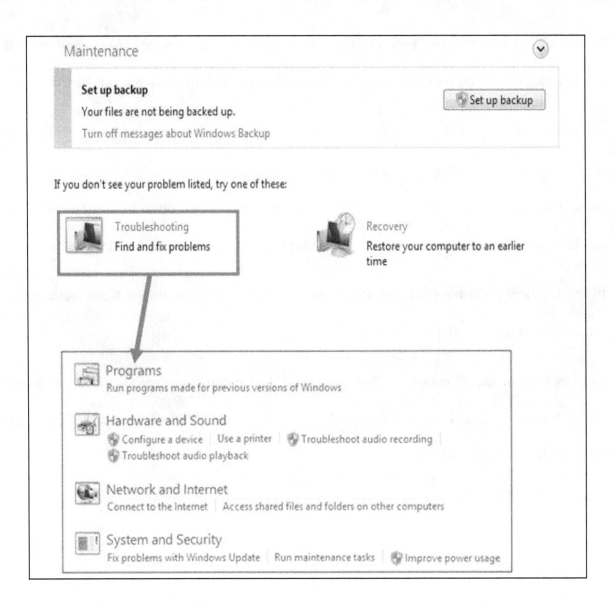

You can select **Connect to the Internet** to diagnose the problems with your internet connection.

Protecting Your Windows

You can assess your Windows 8 and PC's safety with the help of Action Center, one of the most important parts of your Control Panel. The Action Center displays the problems in your Windows 8 main defenses, and it also provides you with the best fixes for the scenario. You can always stay updated with the Action Center's current status using its icon in the taskbar.

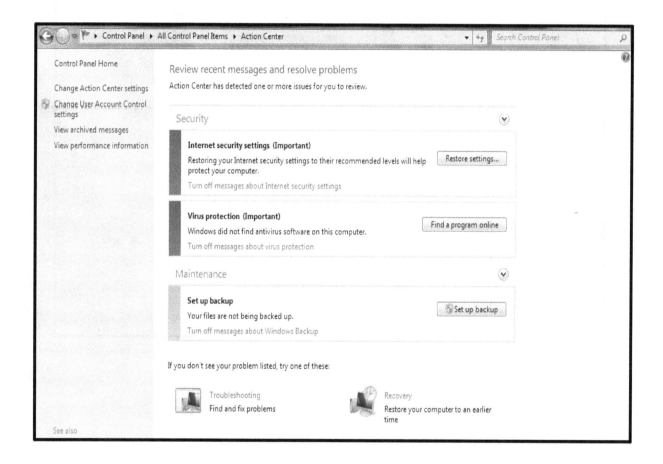

The most amazing feature about the Action Center in Windows 8 is that it color codes the problems. If you see a red band beside a problem, you need to address the issue immediately because the problem is very severe. The yellow band indicates that the problem requires attention very soon.

If your Windows 8 is well protected and is functioning normally, you will not find anything listed under both security and maintenance. When you find an item listed, it is important that you address the issue immediately especially if it is serious.

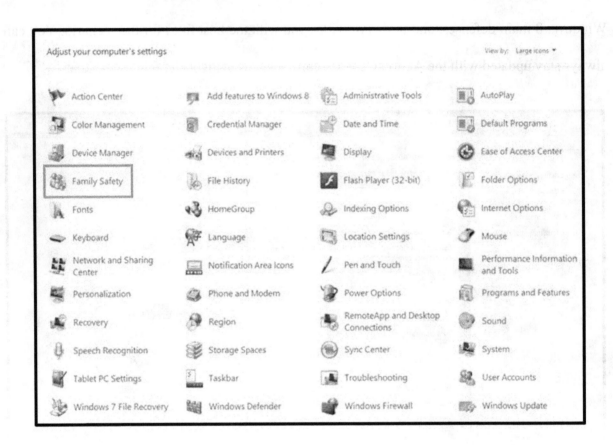

How to Set Up Family Safety Controls in Windows 8

When you click Family Safety, Windows 8 allows you to apply restrictions to one user at a time. This can mean lots of work if you have a number of user accounts on the same PC or laptop. Check out the following figure to know how you can control user account activity using Family Safety.

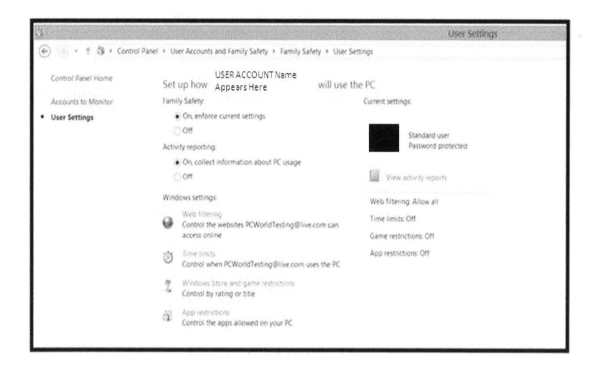

You can click any of the four categories namely **Web Filtering, Time Limits, Windows Store and Game Restrictions,** and **App Restrictions** to make the desired changes. The best thing about Family Safety is that the changes you make take effect immediately.

Data Backup and Restoring Files

As a Windows 8 user, you have a much wider range of choices when you talk about data backup and restoring files. This report does mention that Windows 8 has changed dramatically and you've already seen a few examples on the previous pages.

Those of you who have experienced Windows 8 or have seen a glimpse of this amazing operating system know that Windows 8 not only boots really quickly and jumps out of sleep instantly; the new system actually retains your personal data and settings if you refresh your Windows.

You can try to refresh or reset your PC if you are having problems. If you decide to refresh your PC, Windows 8 retains your personal files, user account settings and the apps that came with your PC. On the other hand, if you decide to reset your PC or laptop, Windows 8 will be reinstalled from scratch. This means your settings and apps will be deleted and you'll only find the apps that came with your PC.

Restoring Your PC using System Restore

If you think that the recent install of an app or program is causing problems with your laptop or PC, you can restore your Windows 8 back to an earlier point. System Restore feature currently is not available for Windows 8 RT.

To Restore your PC:

First access the Charms bar and then tap/click Search.

Enter **Recovery** in the search box that appears on the screen. You can also tap/click Settings in the charms bar, and then tap/click Recovery.

Tap/click System Restore and follow the commands that appear on the screen.

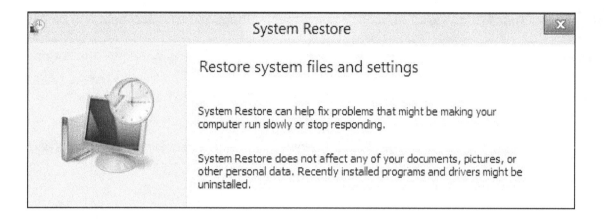

How You Can Refresh your PC without Affecting Your Files

If your laptop/PC isn't working as well as it once did, and you don't know why it is behaving so strangely, you can refresh your Windows 8 without losing your personal settings and files. To do this:

Open the **Charms Bar**, tap/click **Settings**, and then tap/click **Change PC settings**.

Click/tap General under PC settings and then tap/click **Get started** under **Refresh your PC without affecting your files.**

You can follow the instructions that appear on the screen to complete the process.

Note

All apps downloaded from the Windows Store and those that came with your PC will be reinstalled, but apps you installed using web programs or other external media will be removed when you refresh your PC. However, Windows 8 will place a list featuring removed apps on the desktop so you can always download them again later.

How You Can Reset your Windows 8

If you reset your Windows, all of your personal files, settings and user accounts will be deleted. In short, your Windows will be restored to factory settings. Resetting Windows 8 is nothing less than a magic fix, especially when you cannot get rid of your computer problems.

Swipe in from the right edge of your screen to reveal the Charms bar. Tap/click Settings and then tap/click **Change PC settings**.

When you open Change PC settings, tap/click **General** to access **Remove everything and reinstall Windows.**

Tap/click **Get started** and follow the instructions that appear on your screen to complete the process.

Windows 8 and File History

File History is one of the most interesting features in Windows 8. File History means Windows 8 automatically backs up your files stored in libraries, favorites, Microsoft SkyDrive and your desktop.

Even if your original files are deleted, corrupted or damaged, you can still restore all of them using File History. To begin automatic backup of files, you have to first turn File History on and set up a drive for backing up the files.

How You Can Turn File History On

> **Simply hold down the Ctrl button, and use your mouse wheel to zoom in and out on the screen.**

You can open File History by entering **File History in the search box** that appears when you tap/click the Search Charm. Tap/click Turn on to start backing up your files.

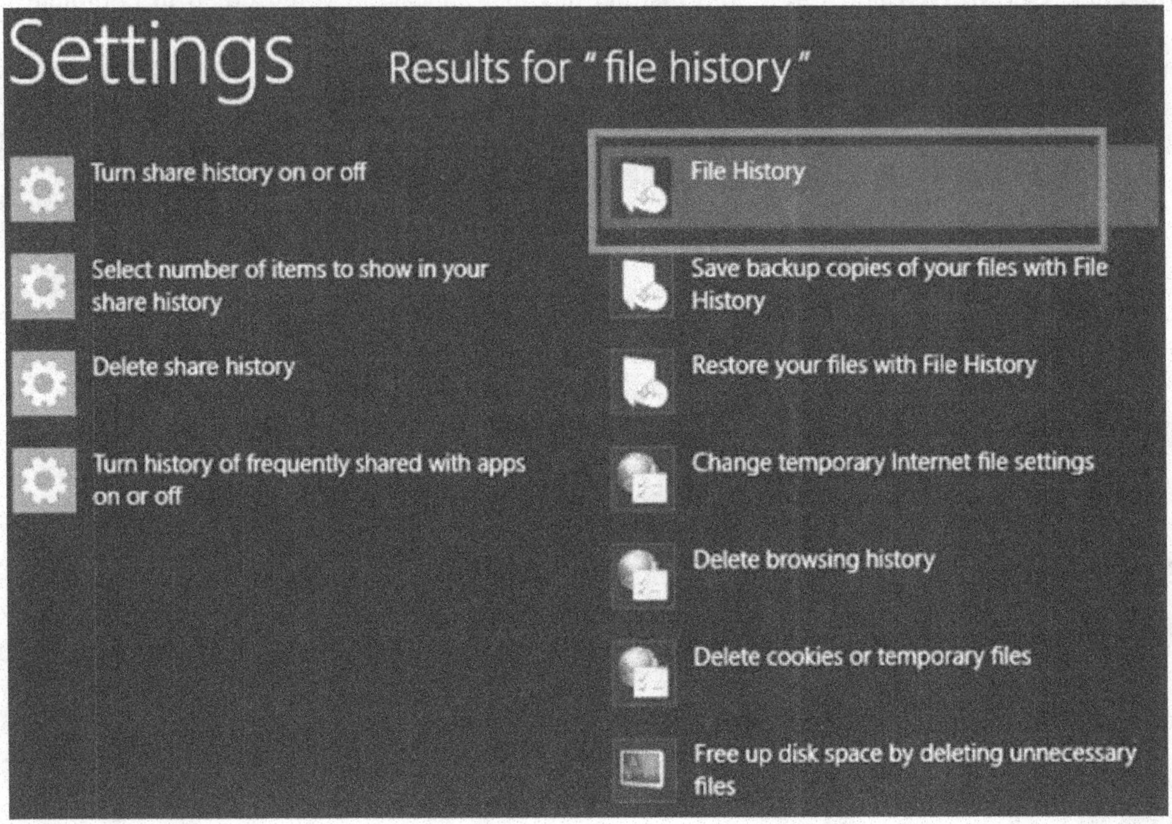

Settings

Results for "file history"

Turn share history on or off

Select number of items to show in your share history

Delete share history

Turn history of frequently shared with apps on or off

File History

Save backup copies of your files with File History

Restore your files with File History

Change temporary Internet file settings

Delete browsing history

Delete cookies or temporary files

Free up disk space by deleting unnecessary files

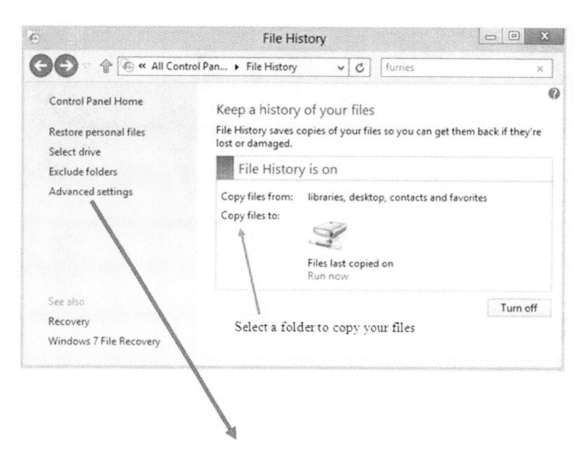

Select a folder to copy your files

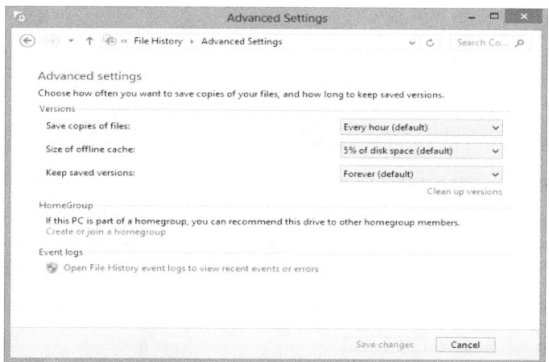

How You Can restore Your Files

Access the Control Panel and then tap/click System and Security.

Tap/click Restore your files with File History to select the files you want to restore.

Your files will be restored to their original location.

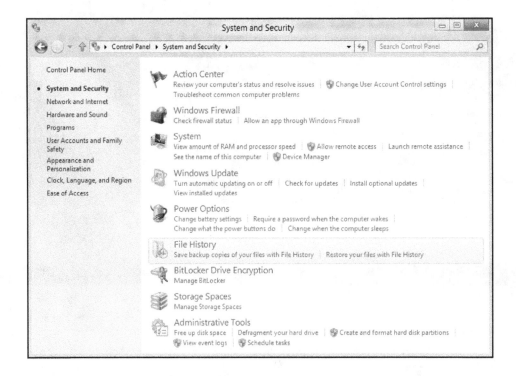

If you want Windows 8 to restore your files to a new location, press and hold or right click the Restore button that appears on the screen. Then tap/click **Restore To** and choose a different location for your files.

You can also restore files using Windows 8 File Explorer. First browse the file you want to restore and then tap/click it. Go to the Home tab and in the Open group, tap/click the History button that appears. You will then be given an option to restore your file or folder.

Chapter Three: Make the Apps Work

How to Use Built-in Apps

Windows 8 apps are software programs you can install on your desktop or tablet. Most of the apps that run on Windows 8 can be bought and download from the Windows 8 store. In addition, the OS comes with some built-in apps as well. For instance, you have the Calendar app along with other user-friendly utilities like Maps.

You can use Windows 8 apps directly from the Start screen and the Desktop. For easy access, you can pin your favorite apps to the start screen and simply click or tap their icons to launch them anytime.

Can You Use Two Apps Together?

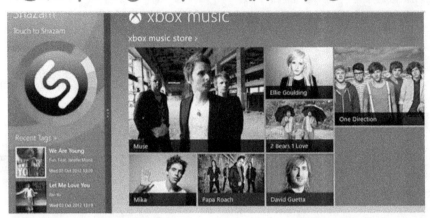

You can run two apps together by using few simple techniques. Firstly, you can use the Alt+tab shortcut (if you are using the keyboard). If you are using the mouse, click the upper left corner of the screen. On the touch screen, use your finger to swipe from the left. All these techniques will allow you to multitask by running 2 apps simultaneously on the screen. This is how it will appear (Shazam and Xbox Music).

Apps can be resized so that one appears larger than the other. However, you can only launch the snap view on screens that are more than 1366 pixels wide.

Switching Between Apps

If you want to move between 2 apps in snap view, you can:

Swipe in from the left (if using touchscreen)

Use the mouse to click on the top corner, towards the left

On the other hand, if you want to switch to a recently used app, you will have to swipe towards the left edge of the screen and then force the app back toward the edge *in one continuous movement*. The apps you have you used recently will now come into view, including the Windows 8 Start Screen. Simply tap the app you want to launch.

If you are using a desktop, use the mouse to click and move down from the upper left edge of the screen to the bottom left corner.

Exploring Accessories and Tools

To explore the various Windows 8 accessories and tools, start by right-clicking the start screen.

Select **All Apps** and scroll towards the right. If you want to launch a program tool, just click or

tap it.

Fun with Multimedia

The Windows 8 comes with a brand new built-in Media Center. However, users have complained that not all multimedia files are supported on this program. There are some alternatives that will help you make the most of multimedia on Windows 8.

For starters, driver compatibility issues were resolved for the most part before the commercial launch of Windows 8, and the Pro version includes the upgraded Media Centre Pro which supports Blu-ray and DVD format.

Playback issues do occur mostly because of inadequate codecs, and you can always resolve these issues by installing codecs yourself. Free codec packages are also available at http://shark007.net/win8codecs.html.

Alternately, you can once again resort to third-party programs to run your media files. You can get various third-party media players with all the necessary codec included over the internet.

Building Your Own Applications

The Windows Appstore is still developing, especially if you compare it with what iOS or Android have to offer. Microsoft has provided some tools for those who want to develop their own apps to run on Windows 8.

For instance, multiple language support is offered on the Windows 8 software developer kit (SDK). If you already know a tad bit about app development and programming, along with languages like C# or C++, then building Windows 8 apps will become easy for you. To get on with your Windows 8 app development, you can visit the Windows Development Center website.

Using Live Tiles

Live Tiles sit on your Start Screen providing updates about and quick access to your favorite apps. To remove the tiles, right-click on the app and go to the menu that comes up at the bottom of the screen.

Here you can unpin the app from the Start Screen, change its size, make it "un-live", and even uninstall it. Note that you can perform these actions on all tiles by selecting them and the right-clicking any one.

SkyDrive and Social Apps

SkyDrive is a storage program which helps you save and backup files on Windows 8. You can find more information about SkyDrive in Chapter Nine. As far as your social connections are concerned, the built-in People's app allows you to view updates and enter posts on Facebook and Twitter.

Wonder how you can use People App for Windows 8? Here are some quick tips to get you started.

How You Can Add Contacts to 'People'

Tap/click People on the Start screen.

Swipe in from the right edge of the screen to access Charms bar and then tap Settings.

Tap/click New contact.

Enter information you want to add to the contact and then tap/click Save.

Remember, you need to have a Microsoft account to use People and removing your Microsoft Account will delete all your contacts from People, Mail and Calendar.

How You Can Search Contacts

There are a number of ways you can get to a contact.

Tap/click People on the start screen and then access the Charms bar.

Tap/click Search and enter the name of a contact.

Tap/click the magnifying glass icon to start searching.

OR

Tap/click People on the start screen and then touch the Home screen with two or more fingers.

Pinch the screen and zoom out or you can click Zoom button ▬ if you are using a mouse.

Tap/click the matching letter and look for the person.

OR

Tap/click People on the start screen and tap/click the contact you want to see.

Swipe up from the bottom of the screen and tap/click Pin to Start

Enter a name for your favorite contact and get all their status updates on your start screen. You can also email, message or call the contact from the Live tile you've created.

How You Can Link Contacts

It is possible that you have two or more contacts for the same person. This is a common scenario these days because most of your friends will have different email accounts along with accounts on different social network websites.

Here is a quick way to link contacts and make your job easier.

Tap/ click the contact you want to link.

Swipe up from the bottom of your screen and then tap/click Link.

Contacts that are already linked will appear under Linked profiles. When you find the contact you are looking for under Suggestions, tap/click it.

Tap/click Save.

How You Can Link Contacts

It is possible that you have two or more contacts for the same person. This is a common scenario these days because most of your friends will have different email accounts along with accounts on different social network websites.

Here is a quick way to link contacts and make your job easier.

Tap/ click the contact you want to link.

Swipe up from the bottom of your screen and then tap/click Link.

Contacts that are already linked will appear under Linked profiles. When you find the contact you are looking for under Suggestions, tap/click it.

Tap/click Save.

You Can Always Stay in Touch With Email and Calendar

Life can get really busy and staying close to family and friends will be nothing less than a challenge. With the built-in Mail and Calendar apps in Windows 8, all your important appointments and email accounts come together, so it's really easy to stay connected with your family and friends - people that really matter to you.

Now you can see all your schedules in one place with the built-in Calendar app. Your appointments will be color-coded and you can actually control the appointments you can see at any time. This makes sure your work commitments don't ruin your personal time.

Here's how you can customize the appointments you can see.

First open the Calendar app and then open the Settings charm.

Tap or click Options to select the calendar you want to see.

You can also mark the important birthdays, business meetings and any special event by customizing screen notifications from your calendar and social network apps. Here's how you can do it instantly.

First access the Settings charm and then tap/click **Change PC Settings**.

Tap/click Personalize.

Under Lock screen apps, add Calendar.

Tap/click Notifications but make sure Calendar is On.

Chapter Four: The All New "Windows Store" – Your Personal Dashboard

Shopping in the Windows Store

Microsoft has recently announced that the Windows Store has passed 100 million downloads.

Let us now have a look what the Microsoft Appstore has to offer.

For starters, the Windows Store is also based on the Metro layout. On the homepage there are

categories of different apps, and the store also features lists of top paid and free apps. Broadly

speaking, the layout of the homepage makes browsing user-friendly.

Exploring and Obtaining Apps

Once you are at the Windows Store homepage, you can enter a particular category and click or tap an individual app to open its description page where you will find a product summary, technical information, reviews, and screenshots. If you want to view your list of currently installed apps, open the charms bar and select **Settings,** followed by **Accounts and Preferences.** Finally select **View your apps.**

Installing apps is easy as you simply have to click/tap the "Install" option on the product page. To try a preview version of a paid app, click "Try". Installed apps will appear on the Start Screen, but you can always unpin and send them to the "All Apps" list, which can be seen by right-clicking on the start screen.

To uninstall apps, swipe down the screen or right click and select **Uninstall** in the menu that appears at the bottom of the screen. You can even uninstall built-in apps like Mail, Xbox Live, and Sky Drive; these have their own section in the store.

Chapter Five: Windows 8 and Security Features

The Internet Explorer 10 on Windows 8 comes equipped various security features not only to protect your personal information, but also to guard your system against malware and other threats.

Some of these features include the SmartScreen technology and the "Do Not Track" web tracking program. For more information, refer back to **"Web Tracking Protection"** section.

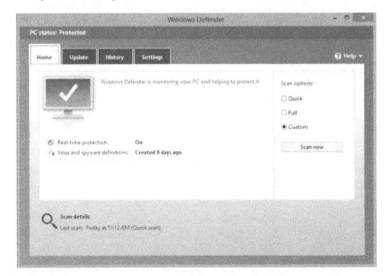

Windows Defender in Windows 8 is always active in the background and notifies you when you need to take specific actions.

To remain on a safer side, you can always run your own scan whenever you want. This is helpful especially if your PC isn't working properly, or you received an email from an unknown sender. You can also use Windows Defender to check for malware or viruses you might have downloaded by mistake. Virus attacks are likely if you download apps from sources that are not reliable.

Windows SmartScreen is a safety feature you must try in Windows 8 and Windows RT. Luckily, Windows SmartScreen helps protect your Windows from malware that is not detected by your antivirus software.

Whenever you download or run an app downloaded from the internet, Windows SmartScreen warns you if the app might be malicious or dangerous to your system.

Remember, running malicious apps can put your Windows and PC at risk. You can use SmartScreen Filter in Internet Explorer 10 to remain safe when browsing the web. The filter warns you if you access a website that has been reported as dangerous.

Chapter Six: What's so new in Windows 8?

One of the most common questions people ask about the latest OS from Microsoft is "What's so new in Windows 8?" Well this new offering from Microsoft is impressing people around the globe and here are some features that make it truly remarkable.

Windows Store

Microsoft's Windows store in Windows 8 is quite a surprise for Windows users because Apple store for Mac and iOS devices has been around for a long time. With the help of Windows Store, you get instant access to free and paid apps. These apps are designed to be used on Windows tablets and touchscreen devices, but there are a number of apps that work quite well even when you use a keyboard and a mouse. What's even more amazing is the fact that you can get free trials for particular apps.

Meet the Windows Store

Make more money on your terms. Discover your opportunity with the reach, flexibility, and transparency of the Windows Store.

Microsoft Account and Cloud Connection

Windows 8 now offers Microsoft Account Integration which means you can use one Microsoft account to sync the same settings and preferences on every gadget that has Windows 8. This means you can sync your favorite music, apps, files and contacts including contact details of your friends on Hotmail, Facebook and Twitter. You no longer have to customize every device to access your files.

Internet Explorer 10

Throughout the years, IE has been under a great deal of criticism when compared to other popular web browsers. But Internet Explorer 10 has a number of useful features which actually makes it one of the most reliable and secure web browser at this point in time.

You will a detailed description about IE 10 in Chapter 11, but for now, let's see the exact reason IE 10 is rated as one of the cleanest and safest web browser. Microsoft's Internet Explorer for Windows 8 has a **'Do Not Track'** feature enabled by default. This means no website will be able to follow your activity over the internet, which is one of the biggest concerns for users that spend a great deal of time online.

Family Safety Settings

Monitoring your kids and keeping them safe when using the PC or laptop gets really easy with Windows 8. You can access the Family Safety feature in the Control Panel and it allows you to block a number of features and apps on your kid's user account. This safety feature also gives you a chance to block certain websites and games.

Web and computer activity reports can also be created for every user account on your computer and you can receive them via email. The weekly report can give a good idea about what your kids have been doing on the computer including web browsing details, how long your kids have been using the computer and more.

Virus and Malware protection

Malicious software and viruses pose a constant threat to your Windows especially when you are browsing the internet. To keep your OS and System safe right from the start, Windows 8 combines the Windows Defender with the excellent security features of Microsoft's Security Essentials software.

Windows 8 Interface

Windows 8 is more aesthetically pleasing and does not feature the traditional Start menu that has been present since Windows OS was first launched in 1995. Windows 8 has made headlines with its new Tile interface as you can now access all your files and folders in an easy way. The live tiles look great on touchscreen and tablets but if you are using a desktop, you can always switch back to the more familiar desktop environment. But there's a twist to the story. The familiar desktop in Windows 8 also has the added sheen to make your experience more rewarding.

Online Storage and SkyDrive

Microsoft has been offering online storage since 2007 in various forms but Windows 8 finally gets online with the SkyDrive app. You can now access files and documents stored in your SkyDrive by signing in using your Microsoft Account. Your settings will automatically be synced to the new device which means any computer with Windows 8 can become your 'computer' just by logging in using your Microsoft account. Online storage and SkyDrive app is an attempt on Microsoft's part to help you access everything you store on the cloud.

Windows Reader

Before Windows 8, reading a PDF file on Windows OS was only possible using additional software such as the Adobe Reader. Fortunately, this is now history. Windows 8 has gotten even better with a built-in PDF that does all what you expect it to do. Windows Reader is rather simple, but it is a good thing considering what you want from it. You can find all the basic functions to make your job easier.

Integrated Social Networks

If you always wished for an operating system that can be linked to your social network accounts such as Facebook and Twitter, your wait is finally over. You can now sync your Windows 8 with a number of social networks including Facebook, Twitter, LinkedIn and Google. The built-in People App in your Windows 8 displays the latest updates right on your screen and you can also post on your own Facebook and Twitter accounts.

If your friend has multiple accounts such as an account on Facebook, Twitter and LinkedIn, all information will be combined and added to the individual account for your easy access.

Chapter Seven: Hardware and Device Compatibility

We have talked about hardware and other requirements for Windows 8 earlier, but here, let's see a few things beyond the basics. Windows 8 actually makes you feel so comfortable with the touch interface, actually the touch feature is as much a part of this new OS as a keyboard or mouse are.

This means Windows 8 runs more effectively and efficiently on touch-enabled hardware and you can see this on Windows 8 tablets. The latest OS from Microsoft supports full tenpoint multitouch and this is not all. You will also support for two-handed gestures and multi-fingers.

Frankly, most Windows 8 users are in love with the touch enabled features. Now, casual web browsing and multimedia experience would never be the same and have no comparison with what a mouse and keyboard can do. Working with an operating system that is touch enabled itself is very exciting because you can take advantage of the new capabilities.

Windows 8 Gives You More Flexibility

Windows 8 gives you everything you need. It combines flexibility with convenience so that you get a great experience using a laptop or PC or a touch device. Your productivity will not be affected in any case and Windows 8 can be taken along practically anywhere, anytime. You would understand this better after you use the cloud connections offered by Windows 8.

Give Your Device a Longer life

Most of you would be surprised to know that Windows 8 can be used on ultra fast desktops and the most modern tablets. This shouldn't surprise those of you who are using Windows 8, but there is something that will make you feel proud of your selection. Windows 8 runs perfectly on low power so you can do lots of work with a single fully charged battery. Now there is no need to compromise on your work and you'll not miss a single deadline. Lower power requirement of Windows 8 has opened the path for the development of many energy efficient devices that are specially designed to work with Windows 8.

Connect and Share Between Devices

Tap and Setup is an interesting feature that is available when you install Windows 8. You can easily connect wireless devices to your PC including keyboard, mouse, speakers, headphones, wireless printers and Xbox without the need of complicated PIN or complex setup steps. Windows 8 also senses wireless devices automatically and makes them ready to use with a simple connection.

The Windows 8 Upgrade Assistant shows you the list of devices that are compatible with your OS. It also lists the items you need to review before you can upgrade your old Windows to Windows 8.

Chapter Eight: How Can You Move Your Stuff on Windows 8?

Moving files and settings from another PC – Windows Easy Transfer

What is Windows Easy Transfer?

Windows Easy Transfer is a useful program that can be used for file transfer and backup. The basic purpose of Windows Easy Transfer is to help you transfer files from an older version of Windows to a new one.

What Can You Transfer?

Windows Easy Transfer moves your files and settings from your old PC to the new one. However, both your computers should be running on a Windows OS that supports Windows Easy Transfer.

You can transfer all of your files including:

Music, pictures, videos, email, contacts and favorites

User accounts and their customized settings

Configuration data stored in Windows Registry (This feature is not available for Windows 2000).

What are the Supported Formats?

Windows Easy Transfer is available for

Windows 8

Windows 7

Windows XP

Windows Vista and

Windows 2000

What Transfer Methods Can You Use?

You can either:

Use an Easy Transfer cable that is available from your PC manufacturer or any electronic store.

Remember, USB cables cannot be used with Windows Easy Transfer.

Use a common computer network that has both your PCs connected.

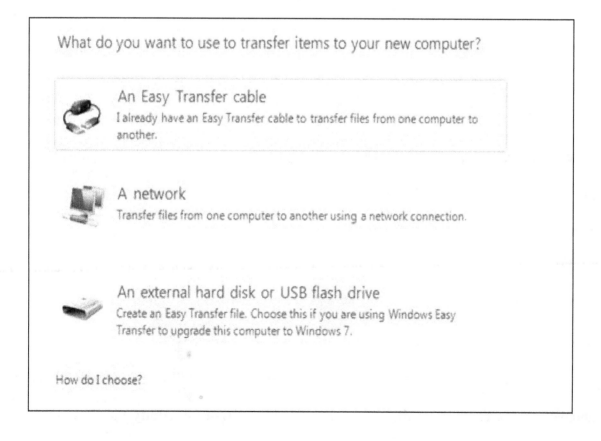

Use an external hard drive such as a USB that is compatible with your PC and has enough storage space.

Preparing for File Transfer

It is always better to scan your PC for malware and other viruses before you start transferring the files. Make sure you run antispyware program to guarantee that malicious software are not transferred to your new system.

Step One: Install Windows Easy Transfer on both the PCs.

Step Two: On Windows 8, open Windows Easy Transfer by tapping Search from the Charms bar. Tap/click Windows Easy Transfer under apps and enter an admin password if you are asked. Tap/click next when you see the Welcome screen. Choose the most convenient transfer method and then tap/click **This is my new PC.**

Step Three: Move to your old PC running Windows 7, Windows Vista or Windows XP and open Windows Easy Transfer. You can enter Easy Transfer in the search box to search for Windows Easy Transfer in Windows 7. The search box appears when you click the Start Button. For Windows Vista, click the Start button, go to All Programs > Accessories > System Tools and then click Windows Easy Transfer. For Windows XP, go to All Programs, and then click Windows Easy Transfer.

Step Four: Click Next when you guided to Windows Easy Transfer's Welcome Screen in your old PC.

Step Five: Choose the same transfer method you selected for Windows 8 and follow the instructions that appear on your screen. Windows Easy Transfer will first scan your PC and then automatically select all your files it can transfer. If you want to modify the files that can be transferred from any user account, first click Customize under a user account and then unmark the check boxes next to the files you don't want to transfer.

Step Six: To see a list of everything that is transferred to Windows 8, tap/click See what was transferred.

Are There Any Problems?

Presently, Windows Easy Transfer cannot be used to transfer files from a 64-bit version of Windows to a 32-bit version of Windows. If you face the same problem, you need to move your files manually.

You need to have a USB flash drive or external hard drive to move your files Windows RT PC. This is because Windows Easy Transfer cannot be used to move files to or from a Windows RT PC.

Windows Easy Transfer does not transfer program settings if both your PCs have different language settings.

Chapter Nine: The Cloud Connection – Your Contacts and Documents are Everywhere!

You Can Do Great Things with Windows 8 Cloud Connection

One of the biggest attractions of the latest OS from Microsoft is that your Windows 8 is everywhere. Just sign in using your Microsoft account on any laptop, PC or tablet and your Windows 8 settings are all there. And, if you share your Windows 8 device with other users, everyone can have their personalized cloud connection by signing in with their Microsoft Account.

Whenever cloud computing gets involved in the equation, you can start your work on one device and finish it on any other device. The cloud stores your files and information and there are no boundaries when it comes to file transfer. You'll be surprised to know that the cloud can store a large number of files including music, photos, games, Windows settings and apps. All you have to do is sign in to a Windows 8 PC and access all of your stuff from practically every location in the world.

Messaging and staying connected with your friends is really easy with Windows 8. You have all the contacts in one place even if each of your friends are on a number of different social network websites including Facebook, Twitter and even Gmail, Hotmail and Messenger. Contact information is readily available as you sign in with your Microsoft account.

Socialize and stay in touch

Add your email contacts, Facebook friends, and more to People

Make it easier to keep track of everyone who matters to you. You can quickly add your email contacts, your social networks, the people you follow on Twitter, and more to one central contact list when you use the People app. When your friends update their contact info somewhere like Facebook, LinkedIn, or Twitter, or you make a change in another account, it automatically updates in People. And when you use other apps, like Mail, you can choose right from this list.

You have a fully updated and connected address book courtesy the People app on Windows 8. So, you no longer have to worry as the People app helps keep track of what's going on with your friends. More importantly, your life is made easier as all this information is available in one place.

Stay Connected to your files 24/7

You already know that your Windows 8 goes everywhere you go so you can now stay connected to your files 24/7. You can be ready to pick up your work where you left off just by signing in from a Windows 8 device. When your files are in SkyDrive, you can access your files the same way you access things on your PC. You only need an internet connection and a web connected device to access your files stored on Microsoft SkyDrive.

What is SkyDrive?

SkyDrive, officially called Microsoft SkyDrive is a type of online storage service that allows you to store your personal files in the cloud. The service currently offers 7 GB of free storage space to all users and you can get additional storage by paying an extra amount.

What does SkyDrive do?

Create Microsoft Office Documents Directly on the Web

SkyDrive apps now allow you to create, edit and view Microsoft Office documents directly on your web browser. You can work on documents created using Word, Excel, PowerPoint and OneNote on your Windows 8 PC that has SkyDrive.

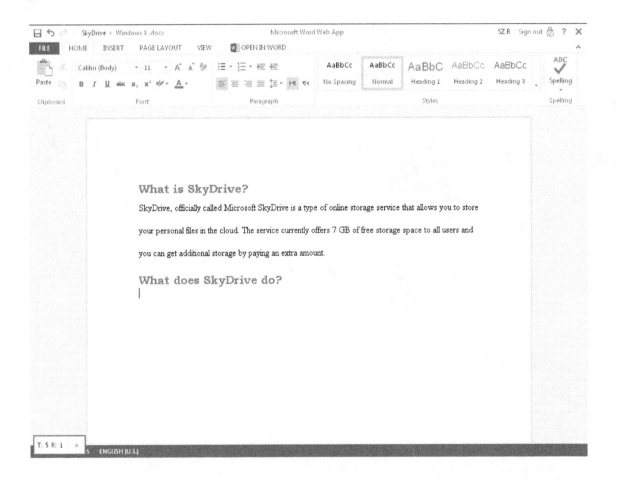

SkyDrive also supports viewing of documents in other formats such as Portable Document Format (PDF) and Open Document Format (ODF). You can also embed your Microsoft Office documents (such as Word, Excel and PowerPoint) directly onto other web pages using SkyDrive.

Work Wonders with Your Hotmail and Outlook.com Accounts

SkyDrive integrates with your email account on Hotmail and Outlook.com and allows you to:

Directly upload your Office documents and photos within Hotmail as well as store your files on SkyDrive. You can then share your photos and documents with other users.

SkyDrive also helps you view or edit documents created on Microsoft Office directly within the web browser.

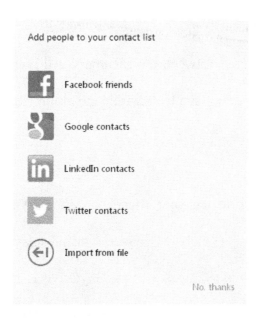

Stay Connected Socially

Microsoft SkyDrive is also a good option to stay updated about your friends on Facebook, LinkedIn and Twitter. Just add people to your contact list to get the most of your SkyDrive. You can maintain a control list to restrict viewing and editing of files by users on popular social networks.

Save Your Search History

SkyDrive integration with Bing's **Save & Share** feature allows you to save your search history on Bing directly into your SkyDrive folder.

Windows Live Group Integration

When you create a group within <u>Windows Live Groups</u>, you will be provided with 5 GB of storage space that can be shared between the members. All members of a group can access, create, edit, view and delete the files available within the group's SkyDrive folder.

Locate and Tag People

SkyDrive gives you a chance to tag your friends on photos you've uploaded via your web browser or Windows Live Photo Gallery. Moreover, it also displays a map of the location you've tagged. The best part about uploading photos on SkyDrive is that you can play them as an automatic slideshow and the entire folder can be downloaded as a single .zip file.

The files you delete on SkyDrive are stored in the recycle bin and do not count in your total storage limit. However, if contents in the recycle bin exceed 10% of your total storage limit, SkyDrive will delete the oldest content first. Your files will be kept in the recycle bin for a minimum of 3 days and 30 days on a maximum.

SkyDrive Desktop App for Windows 8

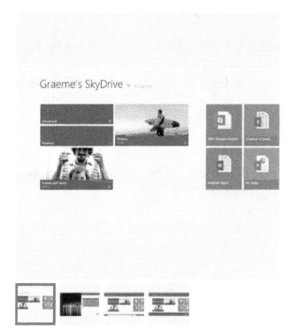

 SkyDrive

Install from Windows Store

With SkyDrive for Windows 8 and Windows RT, your files in the cloud are just a touch away. You can easily view, upload, download, and search for files on SkyDrive. You can share files from SkyDrive to other Windows Store apps. And you can open and save files on SkyDrive using other Windows Store apps.

Note: If you want to download your SkyDrive files on your PC and keep them in sync with SkyDrive.com and other computers, you also need to install the SkyDrive desktop app for Windows.

Features

- View your files on SkyDrive, including files shared with you, and Office files you recently opened.
- Upload files on your PC to SkyDrive so you can access them from other computers or your phone.
- Download files from SkyDrive onto your PC.
- Share files on SkyDrive by using the Share charm. For example, to send an email with a link to a photo on SkyDrive, you can share from the SkyDrive app to the Mail app.
- Upload or open files on SkyDrive from other Windows Store apps on your PC. For example, in the Mail app, you can save a photo you received in email to your SkyDrive.

System Requirements

- A PC running Windows 8, Windows RT, or Windows Server 2012

When you install the SkyDrive desktop app for Windows 8, a copy of your SkyDrive folder is made on your PC. This folder remains in sync with SkyDrive and the changes you make on the web are uploaded to the SkyDrive folder on your PC automatically.

How Can You Transfer Your Files to the Cloud Directly?

If you want to move the contents stored on your PC to the cloud, just copy or move the files to the SkyDrive folder on your SkyDrive folder using Windows 8 File Explorer. You can refer back to page 42 to learn how you can copy files and folders in Windows 8. Files that are up to 2 GB in size can be uploaded to the cloud this way.

You can also the folder on your PC to rename, move and delete files. The changes taking place on your PC will automatically be made on SkyDrive as well.

To upload files on SkyDrive directly,

Go to SkyDrive.com and sign in with your Microsoft account.

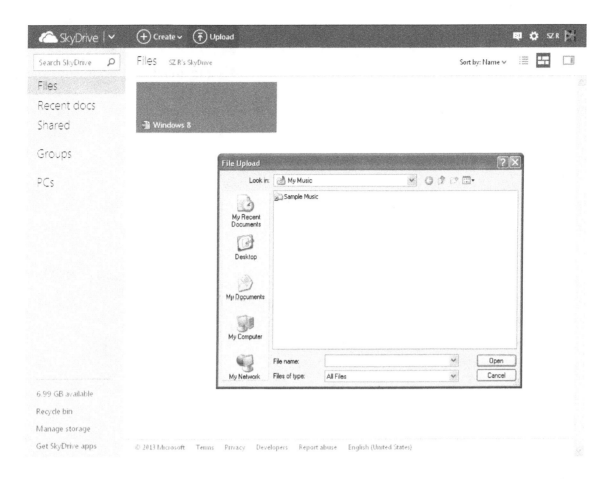

To add files, Open SkyDrive, go to Files and then Click Upload.

Drag up to 200 files into the Drop files area. Make sure you don't close or leave the upload page until all your files have finished uploading. You can also select the files you want to upload and then click Open.

How Can You Access SkyDrive?

SkyDrive is free personal cloud storage and all your files are available from any internet connected device by going to SkyDrive.com. You can also use the SkyDrive mobile app for your phone.

Chapter Ten: Windows 8 for Business

The new and improved features of Windows 8 are extremely useful for businesses as well. You can clearly see that the latest OS from Microsoft is better compared to its previous versions in terms of speed, security, reliability and ease of finding your work. Moreover, its seamless integration with touch, mouse and keyboard makes it number one for businesses that want to make the most of their tactics in less time.

How is Windows 8 Useful for Businesses?

The aesthetically pleasing apps of Windows 8 are very easy to interact and it's more convenient for people to stay connected. You no longer have to worry about the safety of your critical corporate data with Windows 8 security features. Windows 8 offers high class security to keep your business more secure against malware attack. You can opt for additional security with easy-to-deploy data encryption that is available with Windows 8.

Windows 8 allows you to take your business everywhere and stay connected with your employees even if you are on a site, working from home or on a flight to attend your next business presentation.

As you move conveniently between locations, Windows 8 automatically detects Wi-Fi hotspots, if they're available and you are ready to connect to the internet. Windows 8 Professional and Windows 8 Enterprise are a cost-effective solution for employers who want to experience a consistent Windows experience that's as secure as their office PC.

Chapter Eleven: Internet Explorer 10 – Redefine Browser Possibilities

Internet Explorer 10

Fast and fluid

Built to take advantage of the full power of Windows 8 and Windows RT, Internet Explorer 10 starts and loads sites almost instantly. It brings a fluid responsiveness to the web that feels totally new. Everything you want to do on the web is a swipe, tap, or click away.

Perfect for touch

Truly full-screen browsing: Navigation controls appear only when you need them and quietly get out of the way when you don't. Internet Explorer 10 lets you flip ahead or back through your websites with the flick of a finger. Tiles and tabs for frequently visited sites are oversized for easy tapping.

Easy

Smooth, intuitive controls work just as you'd expect. One Box is both address and search bar for speedier navigation. Pin your favorite sites to your Start screen and get to them as quickly as you access your apps.

Safer and more private

Help keep your PC and your information safer on the web with the industry-leading SmartScreen technology that helps protect against socially-engineered malware. Privacy tools like Do Not Track are built-in and can be turned on in one click.

With the new Windows 8 OS also comes the brand new web browser, Internet Explorer 10. With the arrival of IE 10, Windows once leading web browser has become operational for touchscreen devices.

Even though the latest Explorer is the built-in browser on all devices using Windows 8, the strength of IE 10 lies in its usability on tablets. It is therefore safe to suggest that along with being an excellent web browser, the IE 10 provides the best user experience on Windows 8 tablets.

Although popular browsers like Chrome and Firefox still shine on desktops, they simply cannot parallel the dynamics of the IE 10 on Windows 8 tablets. So if you are using Windows 8 on a tablet, IE 10 will prove to be the quickest and long-lasting options as far as exploring the web is concerned. Not to mention, it is fun to use as well.

Basic Navigation

On a tablet computer, the IE 10 is mostly operated by gestures. When you launch the explorer, it always starts up in the Windows 8 full screen mode, where you will have hard time finding the user interface.

Gestures will also help you to look for other explorer features. For example, to bring the URL bar into view, you will have to scroll upwards from the bottom of the screen. Likewise, the tab bar will appear when you swipe downwards on the screen. The tab bar will display thumbnail previews.

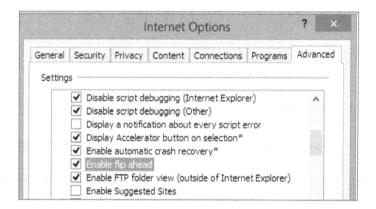

Now the hand gestures are smooth, but you may be displeased with the arrangement of the tab and URL bars. Perhaps both bars should be on the same side of the screen. However, this is just a minor problem.

Additional Features

While the gestures make it easy for you to navigate the IE 10, its "Flip Ahead" feature makes your job even smoother.

Basically the Flip Ahead option allows you to browse the web by continuously swiping to the left, as if you are reading a book or watching a slideshow. The feature automatically searches for any forward buttons or options on a web page and activates them, which means you do not have to click or tap every time to load the next page.

Note that this impressive feature may not work every time. This is largely due to the fact that some pages are filled with inadequate codes and the Flip Ahead feature fails to recognize any options for moving to the next page.

Needless to say that when it does work, Flip Ahead can prove to be one of the most intuitive features of any web browser you have ever used. Just remember that when you are using Flip Ahead, your browsing history is set to Microsoft. But do not worry, as this procedure has been incorporated to help Microsoft improves the Flip Ahead feature in order to expand IE 10's browser possibilities.

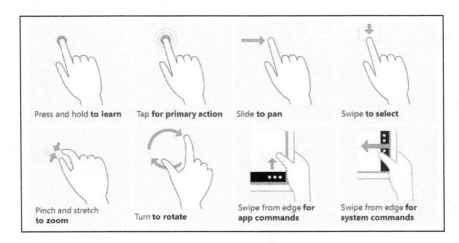

Pinning Websites to the Start Screen

The IE 10 allows you to pin your favorite websites on to the Windows 8 start screen. This feature was present in iOS and other platforms, but with Windows 8, it surely does make things easy for you.

The greatest advantage of pinning websites to the start screen is that you can access them faster, so you don't have to open the explorer and click on the links to access them every time. You can refer back to the section "Customize the Start Screen" in Chapter 2 to learn how to pin websites to the start screen.

Flash Support

Regardless of what the developers said at first, the latest IE 10 does come with Flash support. Initially the plans were to leave out Flash to avoid plug-ins, but developers realized that many websites require the Adobe Flash player owing to the absence of their HTML5 alternatives.

Hence, if Flash was left out, then your browsing experience on the web with Windows 8 tablets would not be as impressive as it now is. Now you have an Adobe Flash player optimized specifically for Windows 8 Metro UI.

The Flash Player will work well with touch gestures on the new explorer, where you can select/copy/paste text with double tap, and you can enlarge a section of a web-page with the pinch-to-zoom option.

This not only means that Windows 8 Adobe Flash Player will be well-integrated with the tablet interface, but it will also lead to a longer battery life, which is nothing short of a blessing for you as a user.

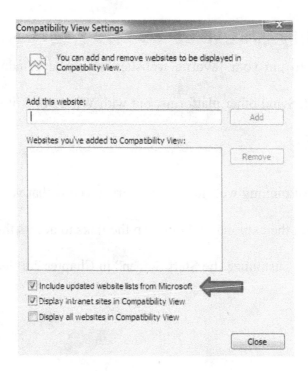

Note that the Flash on Windows 8 will only launch selected websites such as YouTube. Hence, if you are planning to develop Flash games for the internet to be played on Windows 8 tablets, think again. But all in all, adding Flash support to Windows 8 is a great move by the company to enhance the IE 10 navigation experience.

You can find which websites can be run using the Flash player with the help of the Compatibility View. Here is how you can turn it on.

Go to the address bar and you will find a refresh button. Besides this icon will be another button towards the left side. Simply click on tap it to display settings. You can squeeze all websites to be displayed in compatibility view.

On the other hand, you can turn on compatibility view automatically for all websites on the compatibility view list, which is maintained by Microsoft itself.

Note that when you are viewing pages from hard drive instead of the internet, the IE 10 will automatically turn the compatibility view on. This may bother users, especially those who are designing and testing pages locally.

A friendly tip for web designers, if you are designing web pages without setting a DOCTYPE, IE 10 will switch the display of those particular pages to compatibility view.

Web Tracking Protection

The IE 10 has been designed to provide a safer browsing experience for Windows 8 users. In addition, it also guarantees to protect your private information when you visit different websites. This is ensured by the high-quality SmartScreen technology, which protects your system against malware generated by suspicious links.

Moreover, the "Do Not Track" program comes by default on Windows 8. This was developed by Mozilla and now it has been incorporated on major platforms like Opera, Safari, and Firefox. However, these systems do not have this features automatically enabled.

In your case, **Do Not Track** is enabled by default on the latest Windows 8 OS. If you want to disable the feature, you need to select the advanced setup option. Basically this program is a privacy system that protects your system while you are browsing the internet by obstructing websites from gathering and collecting your personal data.

Of course, this feature will have negative consequences for online marketers as they will not be able to place targeted ads on websites. In fact, many online marketers have expressed their distaste over the fact Microsoft has automatically enabled Do Not Track on its Windows 8 OS.

As mentioned before, an advanced set-up screen allows you to enable or disable "Do Not Track". Here is how you can disable "Do Not Track" on your Windows 8.

Start by clicking **Settings** button on the top of the screen, followed by **Safety**.

Select **Tracking Protection**, which will open the Do Not Track configuration screen.

Now you can easily select **automatically block content** or select specific content to block or allow.

You will notice that there is a lot of configuration information, but instead of being an inconvenience, it has been included to guide the users. Note that blocking specific content from web pages, such as advertisements, may affect the overall layout and the loading performance of the websites.

The Internet Explorer 10 on Desktop

You can even run the IE 10 on Windows 8 desktop PCs. However, this version is not as innovative as the explorer on touch screens and tablets. In fact, there is nothing unique about IE 10 for desktop and if you are already using Chrome or Firefox, you will not want to switch to the new Internet Explorer.

If you have used IE 9 and were impressed by it, you will find good improvements in the new explorer, but apart from that, there is little in the IE 10 desktop version that makes it stand apart from its competitors.

The bad news is that you cannot use the 1E 10 as a default program on the Windows Metro UI while having other programs like Firefox to run as your default browser on the desktop interface. This may well be the biggest limitation of the latest Internet Explorer.

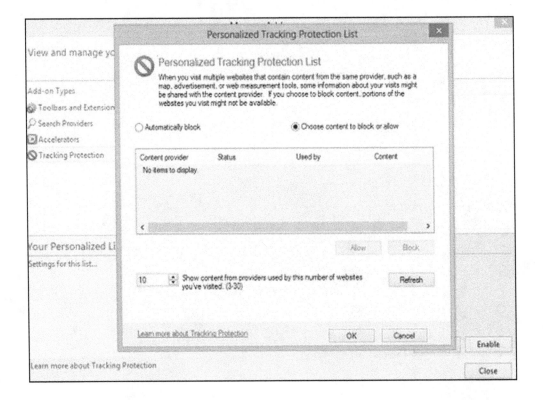

Chapter Twelve: Keeping Your Windows 8 "Up to Date"

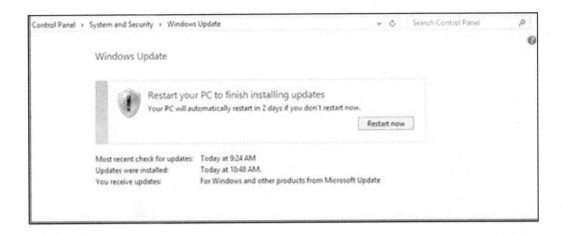

One of the easiest methods of updating your Windows 8 is using Microsoft's own Windows Update program. In this way, you would not have to search for updates over the internet in a fear that your system may not have the latest critical fixes.

Luckily, Windows Updates automatically installs crucial updates as soon as they are discovered. This means your system will be updated regularly and will continue to function well. You can also configure the settings so that Windows Update only notifies you when updates are available.

If you select this option, the Update center will not install new apps unless you grant approval, nor will it remove any applications from your system. When you launch Windows Update for the first time, automatic updating will turn on by default (this setting is recommended). However, you can turn it off during setup.

If you want to view these settings and turn them on/off, you can do so in the Control Panel. Simply launch the Search Charm and click or tap "Turn automatic updating on or off". Alternately, you can hit "Settings" to locate these options.

The Control Panel can be used to activate automatic updating, and you can even determine what your system will do with available updates, and even updates for other Microsoft products. Note that if you are using Windows RT, automatic updating will **always** take place.

Updating Windows 8 Drivers

If have newly installed Windows 8 or simply upgraded your previous system, you may experience some hardware issues after sometime. However, there is nothing to worry about. A basic driver update can fix all these problems and your system will continue to function properly.

For those of you who have still not installed Windows 8, or those who want to re-install it, the **Windows 8 Upgrade Assistant** will come in handy for determining which hardware or software requires an update before you begin the installation.

In addition, if you are tech savvy, you can visit the "Windows Compatibility Center" website to look for the selected hardware and software. Here is how you can update your Windows 8 drivers.

Before starting the process, check if the Windows Update has located any updates for drivers. Of course, Windows Updates cannot locate all available drivers, but still it is a great starting point. To open Windows Updates, once again go to the Charms bar and tap **Settings**, followed by **PC Settings**.

Locate the Windows Update settings menu and hit **Check for Updates Now** and wait to see if any driver updates appear. On your next planned maintenance, Windows Update will automatically install updates.

However, you may have to update the driver manually as well, and for that you need the Device Manager.

To start the Device Manager, go to the start screen and type in **Device Manager**.

Next, in the search menu, select the Settings tab.

Chapter Twelve: Keeping Your Windows 8 "Up to Date"

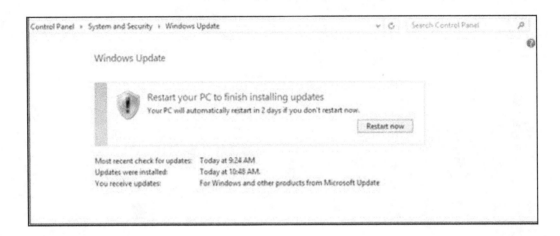

One of the easiest methods of updating your Windows 8 is using Microsoft's own Windows Update program. In this way, you would not have to search for updates over the internet in a fear that your system may not have the latest critical fixes.

Luckily, Windows Updates automatically installs crucial updates as soon as they are discovered. This means your system will be updated regularly and will continue to function well. You can also configure the settings so that Windows Update only notifies you when updates are available.

If you select this option, the Update center will not install new apps unless you grant approval, nor will it remove any applications from your system. When you launch Windows Update for the first time, automatic updating will turn on by default (this setting is recommended). However, you can turn it off during setup.

The Device Manager will now come into view.

Alternately, you can go to the Control Panel and click **Hardware and Sound** to locate the Device Manager.

As far as the updating is concerned, it is rather simple. Once you have located a device for updating, simply right-click on it and choose **Update Driver Software.**

Finding the Right Drivers

It is natural to wonder where you get the drivers for updating in the first place. We will spell out some brief tips for people using different devices. Note that all companies manufacture drivers specifically for Windows 8, but it is always better to use the most updated devices.

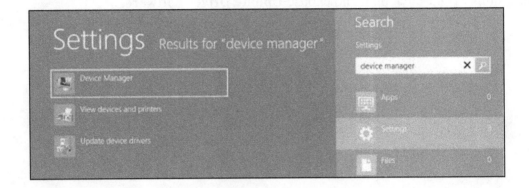

If you are using Windows 8 on your laptop, external drives might not be a problem. However, laptops cannot integrate components from other manufacturers. That is why if you want to update specific drivers on a laptop, always prefer looking at the company's website.

On the other hand if you are using a desktop, you may need to consult the motherboard manufacturers. The company and the model number of the motherboard can be easily seen by opening the system manually. If you are too busy to do so, you can use programs like CPU-Z to do the job for you.

Moving from Windows 8 to Windows 8 Pro

If you have purchased a brand new system with an installed Windows 8 Core version, you cannot get the discounted upgrade to the Pro version and you will have to buy the Pro Pack from Microsoft.

The plus part is that this upgrade hardly takes any time and you simply need a product key; no installation program is required. In addition, you don't have to transfer your system settings, programs, and files as they will remain unaffected during the upgrade.

To initiate the process, go to the **System Properties** dialog box and select "Get more features with a new edition of Windows.

You will see these two options. If you select the first one, you will be directed to a page where you can get a Windows 8 Pro product key and an on-the-spot upgrade after paying some amount. Requirements for the second option are clear enough, and the product key can be obtained from any version of Windows 8 Pro. In this way you can get a surefire upgrade with a product key bought via Windows Upgrade Assistant.

Chapter Thirteen: Tips for Improving Your Windows 8 Experience

It would not be wrong to suggest that Windows 8 grows on you. For example, most users didn't appreciate the start screen and they called for the traditional start menu instead. However, with time as you learn your way about the new OS, you may even forget that there was anything such as a start menu for Windows. In addition, there are a lot of ways in you can improve your experience with Windows 8 over time.

Windows 8 is finally here and you're going to notice that quite a bit has changed in this version. Read through the chapter to know more.

1. Windows 8 will open on its lock screen. If you have no clues about what to do next, simply tap the space bar, spin your mouse wheel or swipe upwards on your touch screen to reveal a familiar login screen.

2. You can access Windows 8 with the help of user name you created during installation. Enter your password to start using your OS.

3. Press the Home or End key to jump from one end of your Start screen to the other.

4. You can use the cursor keys to select a particular tile on the Start screen. Tap/click Enter to select it.

5. Right-click or swipe downwards on apps you no longer need on the Start screen. Select Unpin to remove them. You can move other tiles around if you like.

6. You can click the 'minus' icon in the bottom right corner of the screen to zoom out on your Start screen.

7. If you right click within the block of apps in the zoomed out mode, you can also give the group a name. This also gives you a chance to add another 20 or 30 apps to your Start screen and find the tools you need.

8. Right-click in the bottom left corner of your screen to reveal a text-based menu to access Device Manager, Control Panel, Explorer and the Search dialog box. You can also hold down the Windows key for this purpose.

9. You can swipe your finger up from the bottom of the screen to select 'All Apps' and see a list of all your installed applications. Scroll the various tiles and click what you need.

10. Just hold down the Windows key and I to reveal a power button. Click this to 'Shut Down' or 'Restart' your system.

11. Some of the old tricks still apply in Windows 8. Press Ctrl+Alt+Del, and click the power button to see the 'Shut Down' and 'Restart' options.

12. If you're browsing the desktop, press Alt+F4 to choose 'Shut Down', 'Restart', 'Sign Out' or 'Switch User' options on your screen.

13. If you want to log in directly, select the account you wish to use to log in automatically and then unmark the check-box above the desired account that says "Users must enter a user name and password to use this computer." First click OK and then enter your password on request to confirm it. Click OK to end.

14. You can access the Switch List from the left edge of your screen to see you a thumbnail list of your recent apps.

15. Tap the Start screen thumbnail at the bottom of the Switch list to go home.

16. You can also use Win+C to open up the Charms bar, and then either tap or click on the Start screen charm to go to your Start screen.

17. To change the default program to open specific files in Windows 8, right-click on the file you want to open and then select Open with > Choose default program.

18. To go back to the Start screen from a Windows 8 app, simply press the Windows key. You'll be taken back to the Start screen instantly.

19. You can also press Alt+Tab to see the apps that are running on your Windows 8.

20. If you press Ctrl+Shift+Esc, you can see all your running apps in the Task Manager. This is beneficial for those of you who want to see the extra technical details.

21. Click the spanner icon in IE 10 and select 'View on the desktop' to reveal the full desktop version of Internet Explorer 10.

22. You can use Windows 8 spell-check in apps where relevant, and it works similar to Microsoft Office. If you make a mistake, a red line will appear below the word and you can right-click or tap the word to see suggested alternative words.

23. You can right click on a Windows 8 app's tile on the Start and select 'Smaller' to cut it down to half the original size.

24. Press Win+I and then click More PC Settings to select Privacy. Click the relevant buttons and display information you want to share.

25. If a Windows 8 application is showing something interesting and you'd like to save a screenshot, hold down the Windows key and press PrtSc. The image will be automatically saved to your My Pictures folder with the name Screenshot.png

26. You can also set Picture password for Windows 8. For this, you'll need to copy at least one image to your Windows 8 Pictures folder. Once you select a picture, draw circles, lines, or taps on any three desired areas to set up your security code. To log in, you simply have to recreate the same gestures in the same order.

27. Some quick shortcuts

    Win+C: Open charms

    Win+Q: Search charm

    Win+H: Share charm

    Win+K: Devices charm

    Win+I: Settings charm

28. Win+Z: Get to app options

    Ctrl+Tab: Cycle through app history

    Alt+F4: Close an app

29. Win+Q: Search apps (tip: an even easier way to search apps is to just begin typing from the

    start screen)

    Win+W: Search settings

    Win+F: Search files

30. Win+D: Open Desktop

    Win+,: Peek at desktop

    Win+B: Back to desktop

31. If you press the Windows key + "," (the comma sign) all current windows will become

    transparent and you can peek at the desktop as long as you hold down the Windows key.

32. The Windows key + R prompts the Run command and you can quickly launch apps and

    other routines with a command prompt.

33. The Windows key + M minimizes everything that's showing on your Windows 8 desktop.

34. Simply hold down the Ctrl button, and use your mouse wheel to zoom in and out on the

    screen.

35. You can use the new Windows 8 split-screen "snapping" function to run the desktop and a new Windows 8 Store app together.

36. Just in case you want to get into Safe Mode, first open the dialog box (the Windows key + R) and type "msconfig" (without the quotation marks). Select the *Boot* tab that appears and mark the checkbox alongside *Safe boot* box.

37. Right-clicking on the tiles will pop up with an option to turn the Live Tile on or off on the Start screen.

38. Those of you who want to know what's new in the area of storage, just press Win+W to launch the Settings Search dialog box. Type "drive" and the system will automatically give you a host of related options.

39. You can use the Page Up and Page Down keys to scroll through the tiles on Windows 8 Metro screen.

40. Windows 8's touch interface allows you to zoom in and out of Metro using a two-finger pinch-and-expand gesture. Microsoft calls this the Semantic Zoom feature.

41. You can also select multiple files by right clicking on multiple tiles.

42. Most old shell keyboard shortcuts also work for Windows 8. For e.g. WIN+D reveals the desktop, WIN+R opens "Run", WIN+L locks current user. WIN+E opens Explorer.

43. To change your home page, go to General tab in Internet Options for the desktop IE 10.

44. The Favorites and History for Internet Explorer 10 desktop version will appear by hitting Alt+C

45. To access private browsing option press Windows key + Z in IE 10.

46. Internet Explorer in the Windows UI can work in either snapped or full view. Press F11 to toggle in or out of Full Screen mode in IE 10 for Desktop.

47. If you want IE 10 desktop to be the default version for Windows 8 and not IE 10 Metro, go to Internet options, and then Programs. In the top of this dialog, change "Choose how you open links" to "Always in Internet Explorer in the desktop."

48. To disable the animations that appear in Windows 8, press the Windows key, type *System Performance Properties*, and then hit Enter. Unmark *Animate windows when minimizing and maximizing* option to get rid of animations.

49. You can also access *Sleep* by pressing Windows Key+C. Then click **Settings > Power> Sleep** to put your Windows to sleep.

50. Windows 8 comes with Disk Defragmenter, now called the *Optimize Drives* tool. You can access it by pressing the Windows key, then type *Defragment,* click *Settings,* and press *Enter*.

51. Twitter, Facebook, Windows Live, Hotmail, LinkedIn and Google accounts can be added by opening People and clicking the *Connect* option found in the top right corner. You have to enter account username and password to gain access.

52. You can run your PC on High performance mode and your CPU's speed will never reduce.

53. The Windows Task Manager gives you a chance to disable programs that start with your computer and reduce its speed. Click the *Startup* tab in the Task Manager. Select a program that is causing your system to slow down and click *Disable* to prevent it from starting with Windows.

54. To block websites from requesting your location in IE 10, launch Internet Explorer and tap *Win + C.* Click *Settings > Internet Options > Permissions.* Tap *Ask for location* to turn it off.

55. The Metro view of Internet Explorer 10 has no support for Add-ons. To enable add-ons, switch to Desktop IE 10 and then click the gear/settings button in the top-right corner.

56. If you are using Desktop Internet Explorer 10 press *Alt + C* to view your favorites.

57. In Metro IE 10 browser, click the Address Bar or press *Alt + D* to view your favorites.

58. To add favorites in Internet Explorer 10, tap/click the Pin button found to the right of the address bar.

59. Avoid installing third-party security suites that slow down your computer. You can go for security applications that come with Windows 8. Windows 8 now includes an antivirus named Windows Defender.

60. Right-click at the top of the screen when you are inside an app using a mouse to see your settings for current app.

61. Hold Ctrl and scroll your mouse wheel to enable semantic zoom when using a mouse.

62. Swipe down from the top of the screen to see settings for current app.

63. Right-click on the thumbnail that appears when switching apps, select "Snap left" or "Snap right.

64. Move the cursor to the top left and then move down to see list of currently apps.

65. To scan your PC for spyware and viruses go to Windows Defender and then select the Quick, Full or Custom Scan.

66. To update apps in Windows 8, first open the **Store App** from Start Screen. Reveal the settings charm and then tap/click App Updates.

67. You can use Windows Upgrade Officer to upgrade to Windows 8 and explore your options.

68. To rotate your photos on SkyDrive, open the photos in your SkyDrive folder and rotate them using a photo viewer app such as Windows Photo Viewer. When you close your files, your changes will be saved and the photos will be automatically updated on SkyDrive!

69. You can keep track of your own social updates without having to deal with different apps when you use the Windows 8 built-in People app. You can also share links, photos, and messages without leaving the app you are working with. So if you want update your Facebook status or Tweet something, Open the People app and then select Me. In **What's new**, select a social network to use, compose your message, and then tap/ click Send. If you want to share links, photos, and more: Open the Share charm first and then tap/click People. Select a social network to use, add a note if you want to say something, and then tap or click Send.

70. Keep a closer eye on your email accounts and folders by pinning them to the Start screen. Open the Mail app, then tap /click the inbox and other folders you want to pin. Open the app commands, and then tap or click Pin to Start.

71. You Can Actually Have the Start Button Back. The first thing most users notice when they start using Windows 8 is that their favorite, familiar Start button is gone. There is no need to panic. It's really easy to get the Start button back with the help of some third party and some semi-official offerings. You can try free apps like VIStart, Classic Shell, StartMenu7 or paid ones like Start8. The paid app has a free 30-day trial.

Advanced Options

The average Windows user simply wants a system to help him in his personal and work life with a few simple functions like storing information, accessing internet, social networking, and providing entertainment (music and games).

However, only serious users will understand the changes Microsoft incorporated in its latest Windows, and the OS itself provides you a lot of advanced tools to customize various features.

For instance, Windows 8 has a restructured Task Manager, Control Panel, and File Explorer to help you monitor your system conveniently. You can install third-party apps to perform various functions on the Windows 8, but it will be better is use built-in features like The Group Policy Editor to customize those functions.

Third-Party Apps

As we have already mentioned third-party apps, let us discuss some utilities not found in the Windows Appstore, but they can definitely enhance your experience on Windows 8.

For instance, let's say you simply can't manage the new start screen and you miss the old menu. You can always bring it using any of the several 3rd party utilities such as StarDock, Iobit, Classic Shell, and Pokki. This is only one example of you can bring your desired changes to the Windows 8 using third-party apps, which will subsequently, keep you interested in the OS.

Keyboard Shortcuts

One reason why working on Windows 8 can be boring, especially on the desktop version, is because new users are not fully aware of the new system and using the mouse to operate different programs can be tiring and even frustrating.

To get out of this predicament, you can learn keyboard shortcuts to go about virtually all functions on the Windows 8. Here is the list of major keyboard shortcuts that you can use to bring efficiency in your Windows 8 usage:

To lock your PC, press **Win + L**

To switch between the Start screen and an app/program, press **Win**

To switch between 2 or more apps/programs, press **Win + Tab**

To return to desktop, press **Win + D**

To open the Windows 8 Search Charm, press **Win + C**

Go to Internet Explorer with **Win + E**

Win + K opens the Devices pane

Open the Settings menu with **Win + I**

To bring the Share pane into view, use **Win + H**

To minimize Internet Explorer window, press **Win + M**

Activate the File Search pane with **Win + F**

Turn device orientation lock on and off with **Win + O**

To switch your display to a second display or projector use **Win + P**

Launch App Search pane with **Win + Q**

The Run box can be opened using **Win + R**

To go to the Ease of Access Centre, press **Win + U**

For notifications, press **Win + V**

Go through your system settings with **Win + W**

To access a text menu of handy tools and applets, press **Win + X**

Ina full screen app, **Win + X** displays the right-click context menu

Magnifier and zoom in options are launched by **Win + +**

Zoom out with **Win + -**

To get an aero peek at the desktop, press **Win +,:**

To move the current screen to the left-hand monitor, press **Win + PgUp**

For the right-hand monitor, press **Win + PgDn**

You can capture the current screen and save it to your Pictures folder with **Win + PrtSc**

Press **Win + Enter** to launch narrator.

Deleting Files

Windows 8 isn't very keen to ask you anything when you want to get rid of a file. Whenever you delete something, it sends the item straight to the Recycle Bin. Yes, no confirmation is necessary, something that was very much present in earlier version of Windows.

Unfortunately, things can get ugly especially if you delete something important just because Windows 8 never prompted you. If you want to bring back the warning signals, right click the Recycle Bin and then select *Properties.*

Check the *Display delete confirmation dialog* box in the new window, click *OK,* and this should be OK. Getting rid of warning is as easy as you only have to remove the checkmark once again.

Managing Users

Managing user accounts in Windows 8 works in a similar fashion to the way you did in Windows 7. However, Windows 8 gives you two ways to manage users. The traditional way, through the user Control Panel, still exists in Windows 8.

You can get to the Control Panel easily. Press Windows, X and the Simple Start menu will pop up. Click/tap *Control Panel* to go user account management screen. You can make the changes and then save your selection for the changes to take effect.

You can also access the Windows 8 user management screen directly. First access the *Charms bar* and then select *Change PC Settings.* Click *Users* and then apply your settings.

Chapter Fourteen: Conclusion – What More Can You Expect?

At the end of this report, you will be more familiar with your new operating system. Most of you would be quite excited to use the tips and tricks mentioned here to enhance your experience. The best part about using Windows 8 is that it is much more interactive compared to the earlier versions of Windows launched by Microsoft. Hope you had a great time reading this report and wish you all the best for using Windows 8 on your favorite device.

Check out my other title

Kindle Fire HD: How to Use Your Tablet With Ease: The Ultimate Guide to Getting Started, Tips, Tricks, Applications and More

www.ingramcontent.com/pod-product-compliance
Lightning Source LLC
Chambersburg PA
CBHW080423060326

40689CB00019B/4362